THE BIRTH OF
AFRICAN-
AMERICAN
CULTURE

THE BIRTH OF
AFRICAN-
AMERICAN
CULTURE

AN ANTHROPOLOGICAL PERSPECTIVE

•

SIDNEY W. MINTZ
AND RICHARD PRICE

BEACON PRESS
BOSTON

BEACON PRESS
25 Beacon Street
Boston, Massachusetts 02108-2892

Beacon Press Books
are published under the auspices of
the Unitarian Universalist Association of Congregations.

99 98 97 96 95 94 93 92   8 7 6 5 4 3 2 1

Text design by Karen Savary

Library of Congress Cataloging-in-Publication Data

Mintz, Sidney Wilfred, 1922–
[Anthropological approach to the Afro-American past]
The birth of African-American culture: an anthropological
perspective / Sidney W. Mintz and Richard Price.
p.   cm.
Originally published: An anthropological approach to the Afro-
American past. Philadelphia: Institute for the Study of Human
Issues, © 1976. (ISHI occasional papers in social change: no. 2).
With new pref.
Includes bibliographical references (p.   ) and index.
ISBN 0-8070-0916-4 (cloth).—ISBN 0-8070-0917-2 (paper)
1. Blacks—Caribbean Area—History.   2. Slavery—Caribbean Area—
History.   3. Acculturation—Caribbean Area—History.   4. Caribbean
Area—Race relations.   I. Price, Richard, 1941–   II. Title
F2191.B55M56   1992
305.8960729—dc20   91–41020
CIP

CONTENTS

~~~~~

PREFACE

～～～

What follows was written in 1972–1973, in the immediate aftermath of the Civil Rights struggle and the swift establishment of Afro-American and Black Studies programs in U.S. universities, part of the veritable explosion of general interest (and publication) in the sphere of Black History.[1] It was intended both as credo and as primer. We were troubled by certain polarizations emerging in Afro-American Studies. It seemed that ideological preoccupations might deflect the scholarly quest charted by such pioneers as W. E. B. DuBois and Carter G. Woodson in the United States, Fernando Ortiz in Cuba, Nina Rodrigues and Arthur Ramos in Brazil, and Jean Price-Mars in Haiti, and carried forward by the generation of Melville J. Herskovits, E. Franklin Frazier, Zora Neale Hurston, Gonzalo Aguirre Beltrán, Roger Bastide, Romulo Lachatañeré, and others. We therefore focused on strategies or approaches for studying the African-American past, rather than presenting the results of such studies to date, with the hope of encouraging historians and others entering the field to employ conceptual models that did full justice to the complexity of their subject.

The argument aimed to build on the insights of Herskovits and his peers. But it was greeted in some quarters by a—for us—surprising hostility, accompanied by the charge that it denied the existence of an African heritage in the Americas. It seemed that many such reactions originated in a desire to polarize Afro-Americanist scholarship into a flatly "for" or "against" position in regard to African cultural retentions. For instance, Mervyn Alleyne dubbed us "creation theorists," charging us with exaggerated attention to the cultural creativity of enslaved Africans in the New World; yet his own book reaches conclusions close to our own.[2] Daniel Crowley castigated Sally and Richard Price's *Afro-American Arts of the Suriname Rain Forest*, which develops the conceptual approach in a particular historical context, as "badly overstat[ing] a good case."[3] Joey Dillard found the authors "not completely on the side of the angels," their arguments "controversial if not positively heretical."[4]

Though such theological discourse is less common today, the contention continues. Joseph Holloway, after asserting that the effectiveness of the book "is attributable to its theoretical framework, applied methodology, and analysis of New World Africanisms," concludes that "Its limitation is its failure to look at African acculturation and retentions outside the Caribbean."[5] A recent exchange between folklorist Charles Joyner and historian C. Vann Woodward suggests that the battle line is still drawn in about the same place. In an entry in the *Encyclopedia of Southern Culture*, Joyner argued in a vein similar to our own:

> The process of linguistic change provides a model for explaining other aspects of the transformation from

African to Afro-American culture. What might be called the "creolization of black culture" involves the unconscious "grammatical" principles of culture, the "deep structure" that generates specific cultural patterns. Such grammatical principles survived the Middle Passage and governed the selective adaptation of elements of both African and European culture. Herded together with others with whom they shared a common condition of servitude and some degree of cultural overlap, enslaved Africans were compelled to create a new language, a new religion, indeed a new culture.

It was this last phrase in particular, very close to a passage in our own book, that Woodward, with characteristic "gentlemanly forbearance," objected to in the *New York Review of Books*.[6]

●

Assumptions, no matter how innocent, about what does and doesn't look (or does and doesn't feel) culturally "African" continue to bedevil Afro-American studies, sometimes with a rather bizarre twist. There is a particularly evocative photo of Herskovits himself, which appears in a volume on the history of anthropology, captioned as: "Melville Herskovits holding a West African religious artifact at Northwestern University, ca. 1935 (Courtesy Northwestern University Archives)." In fact, however, the sacred object that Herskovits holds (as well as the stool, the firefan, the wooden implements on the table before him, and the stool directly above his head) were made not in West Africa, but by Saramaka Maroons in Suriname (where he collected them with Frances Herskovits in 1928 and

1929), more than two centuries after the ancestors of the Saramaka were forcibly transported from their West and Central
African homelands. Herskovits, much of whose life was spent
trying to plumb the cultural relationships between Africa and
the Americas, would probably approve of having this Old
World/New World clarification placed on record here.[7]

Nonetheless, during the past two decades the importance of
focusing on *process* in the development of African-American
cultures, of examining different kinds of blends and mixtures,
has gradually become recognized and acknowledged, as may
be seen in works as diverse as Lawrence Levine's *Black Culture
and Black Consciousness*, Henry Louis Gates's *The Signifying
Monkey*, Sandra Barnes' *Africa's Ogun*, or the essays in Holloway's *Africanisms in American Culture*.[8] Even some of those
scholars whose methods we criticize most roundly in the original essay now incorporate greater conceptual flexibility in their
work. For example, Robert Farris Thompson now writes more
of African-American "callaloo culture" (a Caribbean culinary
metaphor for mixture) than of pure African retentions in the
Americas.[9] His student, David Brown, begins his doctoral dissertation by writing of Afro-Cuban religion:

> The creative choices of self-conscious leaders and their
> dedicated constituencies have made possible the emer-
> gence, growth and resilience of Afro-Cuban religions
> in Cuba and the United States despite relentless official
> efforts to coopt, control and destroy them. Afro-Cuban
> religions today owe their existence to a history of gains
> from hard-won struggles, not passive 'survivals,' where
> their resiliency is owed as much to innovative trans-
> formations wrought on New World soil as to the main-
> tenance or preservation of 'pure' African traditions.[10]

Mirabile dictu.

The general shift is epitomized in the work of the Caribbean historian Edward Kamau Brathwaite, who added the following lines to the 1981 edition of a work first published ten years earlier:

> This is why, for West Indians seeking their own identity, a study of the slave period, and especially a study of the folk culture of the slaves, is so important. It is during this period that we can see how the African, imported from the area of his 'great tradition,' went about establishing himself in a new environment, using the available tools and memories of his traditional heritage to set going something new, something Caribbean, but something nevertheless recognizably African . . . It is the thesis of this study . . . that it is in the nature of the folk culture of the ex-African slave, still persisting today in the life of the contemporary 'folk,' that we can discern that the 'middle passage' was not, as is popularly assumed, [simply] a traumatic, destructive experience, separating blacks from Africa, disconnecting their sense of history and tradition, but a pathway or channel between this tradition and what is being evolved, on new soil, in the Caribbean.[11]

At the urging of colleagues and students, we have chosen to republish our original essay largely unchanged. We have updated a handful of references, mainly to our own work; we have in a few cases modified terminology to keep step with current norms (e.g., "Bush Negro" has become "Suriname Maroon," and "Afro-American" has become "African-American" when referring to persons of African ancestry in the Americas); and we have made several minor stylistic alterations. Were we to rewrite it—or to write a parallel piece today—no doubt its form of argumentation as well as the examples invoked would be different; the essay's tentativeness, its frequent recourse to the subjunctive, would be replaced by a freer confidence, and a large number of substantive advances in anthropology, history, and linguistics would be incorporated. Both of us continue to believe in the essay's central programmatic message, however. Because the text itself retains a certain historical integrity and because each of us has carried particular aspects of its argument considerably further in subsequent works, we have chosen to let it stand on its own.

Our original preface, deleted in this new edition, began with an epigraph from Herskovits.

Disconcertingly enough, it is those holding extreme opinions concerning the Negro who sense the opportunity to bolster their particular theses by reference to the fact that Africanisms have been retained in the New World. On the left, the point of view taken conceives the Negroes of the United States as a subject 'nation,' whose true freedom and full citizenship may come only after the establishment of an autonomous Black Republic in the South shall have permitted the fulfillment of the inherent genius of this people. What better theoretical base for such a program could be found than in material which seems to show that American Negroes, under their skins, are but Africans whose suppressed racial tendencies will, when released, furnish the drive needed for working out their own destiny? At the same time, those on the extreme right, who urge social and economic segregation for the American Negro, also vindicate their position by contemplating the Africanisms retained in American Negro life. Is this not evidence, they say, of the inability of the Negro to assimilate white culture to any workable degree, and should not Negroes therefore be encouraged to develop their own peculiar 'racial' gifts—always, that is, within the bounds of the Negro's 'place'?[12]

Those words, written more than half a century ago, are a potent warning still.

We concluded that preface with some related thoughts of our own, thoughts we continue to endorse, and wish to repeat here.

Because this essay deals with the evolution of social and cultural forms among African-Americans under what were, and are, fundamentally racist and unequal social conditions, everything we treat here may be seen to have a clear political coefficient. In theory, one may analyze the domestic organization of Jamaican peasants, or woodcarving techniques among the Saramaka Maroons, or the feast of St. James the Apostle in Loiza, Puerto Rico, without the need to keep in mind at every moment the political significance of one's findings. *In theory.* In practice, just as anthropological research in general becomes each day more significant in its human and political implications, so anthropological research that touches upon the everyday experience and perceptions of African-Americans must inevitably become part and parcel of the ideological ambience of contemporary life. Under these circumstances, it is vital that anthropologists like ourselves make as clear as we can what we are trying to do.

In this essay, we call for "greater analytical subtlety and more socio-historical research," and we have set forth some ideas to illustrate why we consider these prime necessities at this time in the field of Afro-American anthropology. In the words of one of our most honest, friendly, and valuable critics, however, "the need for subtle interpretation should not be used to minimize blatant oppression and exploitation." We agree emphatically. It is also our deep conviction that the nature of oppression, while obvious in its most familiar forms, involves subtleties as well, one of these being the way that it divides and confuses honest scholars by perpetuating suspicion and fear. The test of our ideas and findings, as we suggest in the conclusion, "should rest more with the tasks of serious historical and anthropological research, and far less with their persuasiveness on logical, ideological, or sentimental grounds . . . The inescapable fact in the study of Afro-America is the humanity of the oppressed, and the inhumanity of the systems that oppressed them." That such oppression has by no means ended should be clear to everyone, as it is to us.

ACKNOWLEDGMENTS

~~~~~~~

The first version of this book was in the form of an essay, presented at the Schouler Lecture Symposium, "Creole Societies in the Americas and Africa," held in the spring of 1973. Professor Jack P. Greene and his colleagues in the Department of History of the Johns Hopkins University provided us with the opportunity to participate in that symposium.

Roger Abrahams, Roy S. Bryce-Laporte, Stanley Engerman, Jerome Handler, Franklin Knight, Barbara Kopytoff, Linda Marks, Sally Price, Raymond T. Smith, John Szwed, and the late William Willis kindly gave us helpful criticisms of earlier drafts.

Price's work was supported in part by a grant awarded by the Joint Committee on Latin American Studies of the Social Science Research Council and the American Council of Learned Societies. Mintz's work was completed while in residence at the Institute for Advanced Studies, Princeton.

In the preparation of the present text, the authors were given invaluable assistance by Margaret Collignon and by the editorial staff of Beacon Press. We also wish to thank Andrew Roy, who prepared the index.

INTRODUCTION

~~~~~

This essay offers a general anthropological approach to the study of African-American culture history. In it we discuss the early settlement of Africans in the New World in contrast to that of European populations, and we compare such settlement, viewed as some kind of "baseline," to the forms African-American communities would later acquire.

No group, no matter how well-equipped or how free to choose, can transfer its way of life and the accompanying beliefs and values intact from one locale to another. The conditions of transfer, as well as the characteristics of the host setting, both human and material, will inevitably limit the variety and strength of effective transfers. In the process of New World settlement, it goes almost without saying that Europeans and Africans participated in highly differentiated ways. Though it may appear at the outset that the continuity and strength of transferred cultural materials weighed much more heavily in favor of the Europeans than of the Africans, we contend that a more sophisticated treatment of the content of transferred

1

materials would fail to support so simplistic a conclusion. The advantages of freedom, which the Europeans enjoyed, could not guarantee greater success in cultural transmission, even though freedom made maintaining some cultural forms much easier. In spite of this, we believe the character of transfers and their subsequent transformations may argue at times for greater continuity in the case of Afro-America than in that of Euro-America, considering the extreme circumstances and hostile settings in which the transfers occurred.

There are a few obvious differences between the ways that Africans and Europeans participated in the settlement of the New World. European settlement was undertaken for the most part by groups of colonists representing particular national cultural traditions—English, Dutch, French, etc. Admittedly, such groups often originated in a specific province or region, lending a particular provincial character to the settlement. Thus in many cases it might be demonstrated that Normandy or Guyenne, rather than France, gave a distinctive character to one or another new colony. Enslaved Africans, however, were drawn from different parts of the African continent, from numerous ethnic and linguistic groups, and from different societies in any region. Some scholars have claimed—we believe with good reason—that they shared a certain number of underlying cultural understandings and assumptions, insofar as their societies were related to one another, both historically and by virtue of intense contact. Other unities and continuities of a more specific kind have also been identified, and we shall discuss some of these. We do not believe, however, that those Africans who were enslaved and transported to the New World can be said to have shared a *culture*, in the sense that European colonists in a particular colony can be said to have done so.

Differences in scale of organization, and *in degree* of regional homogeneity, still must be analyzed in drawing this distinction. Although our argument here is provisional, we set it forth, recognizing the attendant risks. A primary contrast, then, one we shall develop and qualify later, is between the relatively homogeneous culture of the Europeans in the initial settlement of any New World colony, and the relatively diverse cultural heritages of the Africans in the same setting.

A second major contrast, again obvious but essential, has to do with the status of the migrants in the New World setting. Not all Africans who reached the New World between 1492 and the 1860s were slaves, nor were all Europeans reaching the New World in the same period free. Yet most Europeans did come as free men and women, or achieved such freedom, whereas most Africans came as enslaved captives and their descendants remained slaves, in some cases for many succeeding generations. To put it somewhat differently, colonization of the New World within institutional lines was a European undertaking; enslavement was a primary device for securing the labor necessary to consolidate such colonization. These differences in status and power meant that many problems of cultural continuity or reordering that were superficially similar took on very different meanings. For example, in many New World colonies, both the European and African groups were predominantly male at first. The essential difference, however, was that the European colonists could influence significantly the migration of women, *both* from Europe and from Africa itself, as well as being able to exert considerable control over the ways that *both* European and African women were socially allocated. Chronic shortages of women hence affected the development of colonial society in somewhat different ways for the free and for the enslaved, as well as for the foreign-born and for those born in the New World, both slave and free.

Since European settlers usually held a monopoly of police and military power, one might infer that it was they who were able to establish new institutions along the lines of their original—that is, European—character. While we do not consider such an inference justified without a good deal of qualification, and while we believe (as we have already hinted) that fidelity to older traditions may have been easier at times for enslaved black persons than it was for free white persons, it is a fact that legal systems, economic systems, systems of education, religious institutions, and much else could be established and developed by the Europeans by means not available to the slaves.

Two points require mention in this connection. First of all, many of the bondsmen in certain new settlements (as in the case of early seventeenth-century Barbados and Martinique) were themselves Europeans or, as was also true of Barbados, Amerindians.[1] In the case of European indentured servants, of course, they and their masters shared much of their past, in terms of language and certain beliefs and values, thereby bridging to some extent the status gap between those in power and the powerless. When the masters were European and their laborers African, however, differences in status and power were reinforced not only by physical differences, but also—most of all, at the outset—by differences in culture. Secondly, the greater diversity we impute to the African migrants did not necessarily mean that the cultures of the powerholders would inevitably survive in more intact form than those of the enslaved Africans they controlled. But the two situations implied very substantial differences in the way that new cultural forms might develop in the New World setting.

The settlement, growth, and consolidation of European colonies manned increasingly by enslaved and transported Africans resulted in the establishment of societies deeply divided along lines of culture, perceived physical type, power, and status. Usually such societies consisted of small minorities of Europeans and their descendants, wielding power over large majorities of Africans and *their* descendants. We are not predicating upon this assertion a model of total separation between the free and slave (or Euro-American and African-American) sectors. In fact, the interpenetration of these sectors poses one of the most interesting and enigmatic questions to be weighed in examining the growth and character of so-called creole societies. But the European masters' institutional ideal was a colonial society in which no such interpenetration occurred, since merging or boundary-crossing of any kind might eventually erode the principles of coercion upon which the whole colonial undertaking rested. Though rarely voiced in any explicit detail, it is clear that the European colonists hoped for the "acculturation" of slave populations to a total acceptance of slave status—and surely many of them believed that proper methods, unrelenting discipline, and enough time would bring this about.

It follows that the establishment of European institutions was not intended to facilitate the assimilation of the slaves to a civil status similar to that of the Europeans, but rather to serve the needs of the European settlers themselves. Though the obligations to "civilize" the slaves were often perceived as real—and even, at times, as morally requisite—it was rare, indeed, that a colonial power supposed that this might be done

by means of institutions that could simultaneously serve enslaved Africans and free Europeans. Important exceptions occurred; but the rule was otherwise.

The enforced separation of the free European and enslaved
African sectors led, almost from the first, to the creation of
social systems marked by different ladders of status, different
codes of behavior, and different symbolic representations for
each sector. The emergence of freedman sectors intermediate
between the European freemen and the African slaves was,
apparently, inevitable; it constitutes one of the most critical
problem-areas in the historical study of African-American societies.

Ideally, there would be no overlap between free and slave,
not even between the lowliest of statuses for freemen and the
highest statuses of freedmen. "Ideally," we say, since this was
not an ideal any colonial society ever achieved in practice.
But since our interest will be directed in some measure to the
particular ways in which the idealized slaveocracy failed—to
the contradictions, real and implicit, in such a conception—
we seek to keep the ideal and the real separate in advancing
our argument.

1
THE ENCOUNTER MODEL
~~~~~~

Discussions of the origins and growth of African-American societies in the New World have usually involved a model, implicit or explicit, of the ways in which encounters between Africans and Europeans occurred and the consequences of these encounters. Usually, this model posits the existence of two "cultures," one African and one European, which are brought into contact in the New World by white colonists and black slaves. Such a model, because of its rather misleading simplicity, then requires that the researcher choose between two neat but questionable "explanations" of the African side of the equation. In order to think of an "African" culture coming into contact with a European culture, scholars have been compelled either (1) to posit the existence of a generalized West African cultural "heritage," which Africans of diverse backgrounds brought to a given colony; or (2) to argue that the bulk of Africans in that colony came from some particular "tribe" or cultural group. We shall suggest that, in either version, this model needs considerable rethinking. The con-

7

cept of some kind of common West African heritage requires
additional refinement, in our view, even though this will inevitably increase the difficulties it poses for the historically
minded Afro-Americanist. Similarly, we shall inquire as to
the factual basis for attributing relative ethnic homogeneity to
the Africans introduced into any New World colony.

We have already suggested a fundamental contrast between
the Europeans and Africans who arrived in a particular colony,
arguing that the former were relatively homogeneous culturally, while the latter were drawn from diverse cultures and
societies and spoke different and often mutually unintelligible
languages. The European colonists in particular settlements—
English Jamaica, French Saint-Domingue, Spanish Cuba,
etc.—commonly came from the same national homeland,
even though their regional origins and their class statuses often
varied. Moreover, in colonies in which Europeans from several
different countries were found, they often maintained ethnic
separation from one another.[1] In contrast, it was not usual for
culture-specific groups of Africans to have been able to travel
together or to settle together in substantial numbers in the New
World. This is one reason why we feel that the Africans who
were brought to any specific New World colony could not be
said to have had a single collective culture to transport. If we
define "culture" as a body of beliefs and values, socially acquired and patterned, that serve an organized group (a "society") as guides of and for behavior, then the term cannot be
applied without some distortion to the manifold endowments
of those masses of enslaved individuals, separated from their
respective political and domestic settings, who were transported, in more or less heterogeneous cargoes, to the New
World.[2]

It has often been pointed out that the cultures and societies of the slaving area of Africa were (and are) in many regards *similar* and/or related to one another, due to common ultimate origins, in many cases, or to centuries or even millennia of intermittent but often intense contact and mutual influence. They are said to form, in certain ways, a "culture area," when contrasted with other parts of the African continent. The late Melville J. Herskovits is the best-known proponent of the model we are discussing and we may take his formulation as exemplary. Though Herskovits's conception of the cultural unity of West Africa was not highly systematic, most of the common elements in terms of which he described it were of a single type—overt or explicit social and cultural forms such as "patrilocality," "hoe agriculture," "corporate ownership of land," and so forth.[3] Increasing knowledge of West African cultural complexity suggests that many of these allegedly widespread or universal West African cultural "elements," "traits," or "complexes" are not at all so widespread as Herskovits supposed. In fact, it seems fair to say that many Africanists would be more inclined to stress intercultural variation on this level of cultural form and to argue that a generalized heritage of the sort Herskovits postulated for African-Americans probably does not exist.[4] Yet we believe that it is less the *unity* of West (and Central) Africa as a broad culture area that is called into question by our criticism than the *levels* at which one would have to seek confirmation of this postulated unity.

An African cultural heritage, widely shared by the people imported into any new colony, will have to be defined in less concrete terms, by focusing more on values, and less on sociocultural forms, and even by attempting to identify unconscious "grammatical" principles, which may underlie and shape behavioral response. To begin with, we would call for an examination of what Foster has called "cognitive orientations,"[5] on the one hand, basic assumptions about social relations (what values motivate individuals, how one deals with others in social situations, and matters of interpersonal style), and, on the other, basic assumptions and expectations about the way the world functions phenomenologically (for instance, beliefs about causality, and how particular causes are revealed). We would argue that certain common orientations to reality may tend to focus the attention of individuals from West and Central African cultures upon similar kinds of events, even though the ways for handling these events may seem quite diverse in formal terms. For example, the Yoruba "deify" their twins, enveloping their lives and death in complex ritual,[6] while the nearby Igbo summarily destroy twins at birth.[7] But both peoples appear to be responding to the same set of widespread underlying principles having to do with the supernatural significance of unusual births.

Similarly, the comparative study of people's attitudes and expectations about sociocultural change (e.g., orientations toward "additivity" in relation to foreign elements, or expectations about the degree of internal dynamism in their own culture) might reveal interesting underlying consistencies. More generally, for almost any aspect of culture one could probably identify abstract principles which are widespread in the region. For example, though "witchcraft" may figure importantly in the social life of one group and be absent from that of its neighbor, both peoples may still subscribe to the widely held African principle that social conflict can produce illness or misfortune (by means of mechanisms which Westerners class as "supernatural," and of which witchcraft is only one variant). We are aware that, in many aspects of life, the underlying principles will prove difficult to uncover. However, scholars have begun seriously to attempt to define the perceived similarities in African (and African-American) song style, graphic art, motor habits and so forth.[8]

On the basis of such research, it seems reasonable to assume that, if the perceived similarities are real, there must exist underlying principles (which will often be unconscious) that are amenable to identification, description and confirmation. In considering African-American cultural continuities, it may well be that the more formal elements stressed by Herskovits exerted less influence on the nascent institutions of newly enslaved and transported Africans than did their common basic assumptions about social relations or the workings of the universe.

In theory at least, Herskovits himself approved of this approach. On occasion, he explicitly suggested an analogy between the "similarities in the grammar of language over the entire West African region . . . [and] what may be termed the grammar of culture."[9] Elsewhere, discussing Afro-American research strategies, he noted that "much of socially sanctioned behavior lodges on a psychological plane that lies *below the level of consciousness*," and he suggested, therefore, that more attention be paid to the study of "motor habits," "aesthetic patterns," "value systems," and so forth.[10] Likewise Simpson, writing programmatically, showed an awareness that "in the acculturative situation . . . philosophical principles and psychological attitudes are frequently more persistent and tenacious [than cultural forms] because they [may] exist below the level of consciousness."[11] Yet in spite of these pronouncements, neither Herskovits nor his students were able to advance very far beyond the level of overt forms or explicit beliefs when they actually tried to enumerate the shared characteristics of the peoples of Africa.

In commenting on the New World situation, Dalby has written:

> It is obvious that black Americans were prevented from maintaining in North America the large number of African cultural institutions and traditional customs which have survived in the Caribbean and South America. It has been less obvious to outside observers however, that black Americans have succeeded in preserving a high degree of their African "character" at the much deeper and more fundamental level of interpersonal relationships and expressive behavior.[12]

We are faced, then, with a growing awareness of the need to define and describe these deeper-level aspects of the African heritage even if we still remain quite remote from this objective. Recent ethnographic work in Africa holds promise for an eventual understanding of the kinds of principles on which such a model will have to be built, though we will need to exercise great caution in projecting current findings backward through time.

An obvious difficulty with our proposal is that anthropologists have given relatively little attention to such matters as cognitive orientations or interpersonal style, and, when they have, they have rarely done it well. But we believe that this neglect has less to do with the importance such concepts ought to have in cultural description (ethnography) than with the poverty of our conceptual tools. Our lack of the intimate knowledge of a society needed to describe a people's concepts of determinism or aesthetics, for instance, contrasts sharply with our ability to analyze an anthropologically more conventional subject, such as their patterns of residence. If there has been a tendency, then, to define the similarities among West African cultures and societies in terms of less abstract elements, we feel that this has been very much a function of the nature of traditional anthropological concerns.

We do not propose to deal with the intellectual history of American anthropology, but perhaps it is fair to note that Herskovits, the distinguished pioneer anthropologist of Afro-America in the United States, was trained in North American historical anthropology. This school placed heavy—and justifiable—emphasis upon the retrieval of the past, particularly among North American Indian peoples. Such scholarship subscribed enthusiastically to the development of techniques for the classification of aspects of culture, and the geographical description of similarities and differences among "culture areas."[13] Early studies of the indigenous peoples of North America, for example, paid much attention to food-getting techniques and principal foods, and divided up the continent into food and environmental regions. Herskovits's initial studies of Africa were devoted to defining and describing its "culture areas," in particular the so-called "East African cattle area."[14] In later work he gave careful attention to the utility of classifying culture in terms of elements, complexes, areas, etc.[15] It is neither our intention to ignore the importance of such research, nor to claim that scholars such as Herskovits and Kroeber were unaware of the limitations of their methodology. But it seems to us that it was inevitable that such work might lead to a somewhat mechanical view of culture and deemphasize processes of change and diversification. Herskovits himself often discussed these processes in a general fashion and was one of the leading figures in the development of a theory of acculturation intended to account for the nature of change.[16] But the classificatory tendency repeatedly reasserted itself in his programmatic papers,[17] and the task of combining a theory of change with a system of culture classification for Afro-America still remains to be carried out.

However one may choose to define a generalized African "heritage" shared by the slaves transported to any New World colony, we have already indicated our reservations about treating it as "a culture." We conceive of culture as being closely tied to the institutional forms which articulate it. In contrast, the notion of a shared African heritage takes on meaning only in a comparative context, when one asks what, if any, features the various cultural systems of West and Central Africa may have had in common. From a transatlantic perspective, those deep-level cultural principles, assumptions, and understandings which were shared by the Africans in any New World colony— usually, an ethnically heterogeneous aggregate of individuals—would have been a limited though crucial resource. For they could have served as a catalyst in the processes by which individuals from diverse societies forged new institutions, and could have provided certain frameworks within which new forms could have developed. We shall argue later, however, that the probable importance of such generalized principles notwithstanding, the Africans in any New World colony in fact became a *community* and began to share a *culture* only insofar as, and as fast as, they themselves created them.

We have already suggested that there is a second shorthand way of dealing with the ethnic heterogeneity of Africans, within the same bipartite model of culture contact. It postulates a connection between some particular African people and some New World colony or society and argues that the bulk of the African content of the New World culture in question is traceable to that specific African society: Suriname or Jamaica to the Ashanti, Haiti to the Dahomeans, and so forth. All too often, however, the historical connections are simply inferred from a small number of formal similarities, with lexical items, for example, playing a major role in "documenting" alleged relationships. The dangers of comparing the cultures of contemporary Jamaica and contemporary Ashanti should be fairly obvious; so are the difficulties in comparing what is known of the culture of the slaves in colonial Jamaica with what can be retrieved historically concerning the Ashanti peoples of the eighteenth century.

It seems self-evident that such comparative studies no longer can ignore the need to demonstrate historical connection (in the sense that historians and historically minded ethnologists would use the term). Certainly the presence of some item of behavior among both contemporary Jamaicans and contemporary Ghanaians cannot be taken as proof of such connection. In this regard, it does not surprise us that recent studies which begin with slave provenience and demography (rather than with historical connections inferred from cultural similarities) tend to suggest that the slaves transported to any given colony were more ethnically heterogeneous than had previously been believed. In Haiti, for example, there are now quantitative indications that slaves from Central Africa may actually have outnumbered those from Dahomey.[18] In *The Atlantic Slave Trade: A Census*, Curtin, depending heavily upon Debien, concludes that almost half of the total slave imports to Saint-Domingue in the eighteenth century came from Angola, and only much smaller percentages from other regions.[19] Girod, also relying on Debien, comes to the following conclusions: in the period 1756 to 1767, one-third of the slaves in the trade to Saint-Domingue were "Congos," one-fourth "Aradas," one-fifth "Bambaras and Senegalese," and one-sixth "Nagos and Ibos." Between 1780 and 1792, he continues, one-sixth were "Congos," while another one-sixth consisted of slaves from the Slave Coast, Nigeria, and Dahomey.[20] Fouchard questions the tendency to reason backward to Dahomey from an analysis of *vodoun* as follows:

> The hypothesis is attractive, but it does not stand up. It is contradicted among other things by the details, for the plantation inventories attest on the one hand to numerical predominance of Congolese among runaways and, on the other, give no evidence in the peopling of Saint-Domingue—and in no period—of substantial importations of Dahomeans, but rather of Aradas in general, far from being limited to Dahomey, which was, by the way, rather hostile to the trade.[21]

Likewise, in Suriname, research over the last two decades has revealed that there was far greater ethnic heterogeneity and a very different ethnic balance than had previously been assumed. It had been customary in studies of the African heritage in Suriname to stress Guinea Coast (and particularly Gold Coast) proveniences almost to the exclusion of the Bantu-speaking region. Our quantitative data suggest, however, that slaves from Loango/Angola predominated over those from the Gold Coast at almost every period of the slave trade. In the case of Suriname, as in that of Haiti, such findings qualify long-cherished historical beliefs, which were based in large part on inference from perceived cultural similarities.[22]

We would note one final problem with the model that posits a single African culture as the source for a particular New World tradition. The holistic concept of culture implied in it has the effect of masking the processes implicit in both the continuities and discontinuities between Africa and the Americas. To assume that the slaves in any colony were somehow committed culturally to one or another path of development both evades the empirical question of what really happened and masks the central theoretical issue of how cultures change. For example, to attribute the form of *vodoun* initiation rites to Dahomey[23] might be justified, on a provisional level. But on another, more interesting level, we still face the question of which elements of the ritual were faithfully transmitted, which lost, which modified, and by what processes, so that the Haitian rite of today may be understood for what it is: a truly Haitian innovation, constructed in particular ways and under particular circumstances by particular enslaved Africans, and perpetuated by succeeding generations—doubtless, in ever-changing form—for more than two centuries.

The tendency to assume initial cultural homogeneity among the enslaved in a particular colony nevertheless persists. Here are examples. G. Hall writes, "The West African brought with him complex ideas about property. In Dahomey, *which had the greatest cultural influence in St. Domingue,* everything belonged, in theory, to the king" (emphasis added).[24] Hurbon goes further:

But Africa is still so evident in America that one could speak of the existence of three Americas, one white, one Indian and, finally, black America. In North America, for instance, one can find in the Gullah Islands and in Virginia, the predominance of Fanti-Ashanti cultures; in New Orleans, Dahomean and Bantu culture; in Central America, Yoruba culture; and in Haiti and Northern Brazil, that of Dahomean (Fon) culture; in Jamaica, and the Barbadian Islands

[*sic*] and Saint Lucia, that of the Kromonti of the Gold
Coast; in French and Dutch Guiana, that of Fanti-
Ashanti.[25]

Maps tracing alleged lines of cultural influence from particular
African regions to particular New World colonies are still pop-
ular among Afro-Americanists,[26] though it seems increasingly
clear that they involve risky oversimplifications.

We have suggested that much of the problem with the traditional model of early African-American culture history lies
in its view of culture as some sort of undifferentiated whole.
Given the social setting of early New World colonies, the
encounters between Africans from a score or more different
societies with each other, and with their European overlords,
cannot be interpreted in terms of two (or even many different)
"bodies" of belief and value, each coherent, functioning, and
intact. The Africans who reached the New World did not
compose, at the outset, *groups*. In fact, in most cases, it might
even be more accurate to view them as *crowds*, and very heterogeneous crowds at that. Without diminishing the probable
importance of some core of common values, and the occurrence of situations where a number of slaves of common origin
might indeed have been aggregated, the fact is that these were
not *communities* of people at first, and they could only become
communities by processes of cultural change. What the slaves
undeniably shared at the outset was their enslavement; all—
or nearly all—else had to be *created by them*. In order for
slave communities to take shape, normative patterns of behavior had to be established, and these patterns could be created only on the basis of particular forms of social interaction.

While immense quantities of knowledge, information, and
belief must have been transported in the minds of the enslaved,

they were not able to transfer the human complement of their traditional institutions to the New World. Members of ethnic groups of differing status, yes; but different status systems, no. Priests and priestesses, yes; but priesthoods and temples, no. Princes and princesses, yes; but courts and monarchies, no. In short, the personnel responsible for the orderly perpetuation of the specific institutions of African societies were not (in any instance known to us) transferred intact to the new settings. (We repeat that the same problem was faced, though in most cases to a different degree, by the European migrants as well.) Thus the organizational task of enslaved Africans in the New World was that of creating institutions—institutions that would prove responsive to the needs of everyday life under the limiting conditions that slavery imposed upon them.

It is in delineating the difference between such institutions and the cultural materials of African origin that could form part of African-American life that the distinction between what is "social" and what is "cultural" becomes relevant. For some years now, the importance of this distinction to the study of African-American culture history has been sporadically pointed out on a programmatic level. Herskovits, for instance, noted that in acculturation studies "it must always be borne in mind that the carriers [of culture] themselves are the crucial elements." M. G. Smith discusses more fully the fact that "social structure is embodied in cultural process . . . [and] vice versa," adding that "the study of African heritage [in the New World] in purely cultural terms is not adequately conceived and cannot by itself reveal the processes and conditions of acculturation. Thus, if acculturation, rather than the simple identification of elements as African or other, is the aim of such study, we must study the relevant social conditions equally and simultaneously." We do not believe, however, that enough researchers have taken full advantage of these insights in their substantive studies.[27]

We might illustrate the difference between these terms by an example. The Africans who were imported into the New World came from groups speaking many different languages and had no single common language to employ among themselves. Some or many may have been bilingual or even trilingual, and some undoubtedly found in the new setting a few others with whom they could converse in a familiar language. Yet we can assume with confidence that the *initial* aggregates of slaves in particular New World enterprises usually did not constitute speech communities. Often, the languages in which slaves and masters communicated were pidgin or trade languages, that is, languages with reduced grammars and lexicons, used for specialized activities (such as trade) involving groups with no language in common. There is no consensus as to whether such languages were created in the New World or based ultimately on pidgins spoken in West Africa.[28] Nonetheless, it is clear that the first language of communication between masters and slaves would have been a specialized language of this kind. This same language would commonly become what the slaves spoke among themselves in the same setting, whether or not some of them had spoken this same pidgin or a different one in Africa, and whether or not it was learned before or during enslavement.

Soon after the slave settlements had begun to grow in the New World, the various African languages spoken by their inhabitants would, in the absence of a continuing speech community, begin to fall into disuse (except in special ritual settings), to be supplanted by a pidgin. Children born to slave mothers would learn the pidgin spoken by their parents as their first or native language, and in the process the pidgin would expand lexically to serve the new expressive functions of a language no longer narrowly specialized. At this stage, once the language has become the native idiom of a speaking group, it is no longer a "pidgin" but a "creole." The distinction we employ here is based on a sociological, not a linguistic, criterion, though linguistic criteria also may be utilized to clarify the difference.

We feel it important to stress this distinction between a language's "social" (or social-relational) and "cultural" dimensions. True, these are simply different ways of looking at the same phenomenon. But these different perspectives call into question different problems. The content and structure of a creole language, its syntax, phonology, lexicon, and morphology, as well as the history of its various features, constitute the subject matter of one set of research questions. The ways in which the language is used, by whom, and under what circumstances raise a quite different set. By no means do we suppose that all problems connected with the study of such a language can be grouped neatly under a "cultural" or "social-relational" rubric. But the failure to employ these different perspectives may conceal a number of issues that lend themselves to analysis only if the distinction is taken into account. We want to know not only how a particular language, as language, assumed a systematic and distinctive shape, in terms of its linguistic character, but also by what social processes such a language became standardized, was taught to newly imported slaves, could be enriched by new experiences, invested with new symbolic meanings, and attached to status differences. We would suggest, in fact, that the first set of questions cannot really be entirely resolved without reference to the second, because language as such does not take on its characteristic shape without reference to such sociological features as the number of speakers involved, the context in which communication occurs (or does not occur), the purposes to which such communication is put, and the like.[29] Treating culture as a list of traits or objects or words is to miss the manner in which social relations are carried on through it— and thus to ignore the most important way in which it can change or be changed.

2
SOCIOCULTURAL CONTACT AND FLOW IN SLAVE SOCIETIES

~~~~~~

The distinction between a cultural and a social perspective returns us to the difficulties created by an overly holistic view of culture. We have emphasized the extent to which we believe that the slaves were confronted with the need to create new institutions to serve their everyday purposes. We are defining "institution" as any regular or orderly social interaction that acquires a normative character, and can hence be employed to meet recurrent needs. Thus broadly defined, a particular form of marriage, a particular religious cult, a particular pattern for establishing friendships, a particular economic relationship that is normative and recurrent—all would be examples of institutions. It should be clear that, thus defined, the institutions which undergird and articulate a society differ greatly in their extent and nature. In contemporary American society, for instance, one may with some justice describe both the monogamous nuclear family and the national system of banking as "institutions." What such institutions share is, we think, expressed in rudimentary fashion by our definition. But what makes them vastly different has to do with matters of scale, or span, among other things.

In the special context of early New World slavery, only certain types of institutions could be developed by the slaves: those limited in their scope to the slave group, or those which served as various kinds of links or bridges between the slaves and the free. For our purposes, we may conceive of the institutions created by the slaves as taking the form of a series of concentric circles—the image is not, in fact, particularly apt—only impinging upon the society of free men at special points and in specific ways.

We believe that the monopoly of power wielded by the Europeans in slave colonies strongly influenced the ways in which cultural and social continuities from Africa would be maintained, as well as the ways in which innovations could occur. But we must also stress the problems faced by the master classes in controlling the slaves, and in satisfying the objectives for which slave-based plantation economies were designed. These problems were of many kinds, originating in the competition among different colonies of the same power for markets and privileges in the metropolis, in the recurrent need for capital to expand or maintain plantation operations, in the chronic "shortages" of slave labor, and in the struggles between metropolitan and colonial classes. We cannot deal with this wide variety of problems and, in fact, to try to do so would deflect us from our objective. We must also set aside any serious consideration of slavery in urban settings, which we believe poses a whole set of somewhat different problems.

Some of the problems faced by the colonial system, however, were experienced on a very local level—on the plantations in particular—and can be seen as emerging from central contradictions within the plantation system itself.[1] These problems definitely are our concern, because they have a great deal to do with the ways in which new social and cultural systems were established and grew in the colonies, and with the opportunities the slaves had to contrive and to maintain their own ways of life.

The central such contradiction emerged in the interaction between the African-American slave majorities and the Euro-American free minorities in each colony. Slaves were defined legally as property; but, being human, they were called upon to act in sentient, articulate, and human ways: the slaves were not animals, even if the barbarities visited upon them were inhuman.[2] The often unquestioning acceptance by the masters of their right to treat the slaves as if they were not human rationalized the system of control. In practice, however, it is abundantly clear that the masters did recognize that they were dealing with fellow humans, even if they did not want to concede as much. Animals cannot learn to speak a new language, to employ tools and machinery in the manufacture of sugar, to direct crews of their fellows in completing a task, to nurse the sick, cook elaborate dinners, compose dances and verse—or, for that matter, to become adept in ridiculing with impunity the inanities of those who abuse them. Nor do animals organize resistance, poison their oppressors, lead revolutions, or commit suicide to escape their agonies. A literature produced over centuries, in a dozen European languages, attests throughout to the implicit recognition by the masters of the humanity of the slaves, even in instances where the authors seem most bent upon proving the opposite.[3]

This is the core contradiction of New World slavery, and it appears to have been manifest in endless encounters between the enslaved and the free. Without taking careful notice of this contradiction, we cannot analyze adequately the ways in which new cultures and societies took their shape under slavery, or the really obvious fact that slavery, as the basic social institution in Afro-America, influenced the free as much as it did the unfree. Once having taken it into account, however, the social forms that linked the slaves to each other, and that were developed to regulate the encounters between enslaved and free people, are informed with entirely different meaning. The conception of a society divided into two hermetically sealed sectors can be seen for what it really was: the masters' ideal, never achieved. And the conception of slaves as mindless automatons, simultaneously trained to deny their own humanity, while being called upon continuously to respond in human ways to the demands the system made upon them, is exposed in all of its mythical character.[4]

The variety and nature of encounters between the slaves and the free were manifold. Simply to get the job done, slaves had to be given different responsibilities, as craftsmen, as "drivers," as animal tenders, as watchmen, etc. A surprisingly complex system of internal differentiation, based on sex, age, intelligence, experience, force of will, talent, and reliability, typified every plantation enterprise. Slaves ministered to their own sick, cultivated inferior plantation land to grow their own food supply, fished and trapped delicacies for their masters' tables and their own, built their houses, and made the furniture and utensils employed in them. Not only were they the "brute labor" that kept the canefields in cultivation, but also the barrelmakers and wheelwrights, the carpenters and mechanics, the cooks and coachmen of the plantation as well. Many of these tasks could be carried out with only minimum contact with the European masters, but others called for frequent, sometimes recurrent, or even uninterrupted social interaction with those who held power. The principal avenue of encounter, then, was that created by the communication and delegation of command. Though power originated at the top of the system, it could not be applied without taking into account the nature of *response*. We need to take care in discussing this aspect of the problem. Over time, to be sure, and from case to case, the character of response varied. We are unable to do more than to point to the complexity of this issue here, and to stress that our tentative assertions must be refined, confirmed, or disproved by particularistic research. Basic to our view is the idea that the system itself, since it was rooted in inherited inequality, produced conflict as an integral feature of continuing control, whatever the nature of adjustment or accommodation between slaves and masters.

Response came from the slaves; and it was modified by genuine incomprehension, by feigned ignorance, by real illness and by malingering, by various modes of active and passive resistance. It seems entirely likely that, throughout, it involved give and take, and that the masters (as well as the slaves) were quite aware of it. In effect, the masters' monopoly of power was constrained not only by their need to achieve certain results, in terms of production and profit, but also by the slaves' clear recognition of the masters' *dependence* upon them. This dependence was profoundly affected, of course, by the masters' ability (and readiness) to torture and kill, to separate kinsmen forcibly, to deprive individuals of various needed goods and services and, above all, to employ both threats and the technique of "examples" to exact conformance. But we should not be blinded by these realities to the absolute needs of owners, overseers, accountants, and bookkeepers to achieve and maintain certain minimal levels of performance. The whip may have been the principal technique for this purpose, but it could not be, and never was, the only such technique.

Nor was the day-to-day performance of field and technical labor the only objective of the plantation. Many additional tasks "naturally" became the conventional responsibility of the slaves, from nursing the infants of the master's family to cooking his food. These additional tasks brought individual slaves into more regular and intimate contact with the free group; once again, these were relationships in which the power of the free over the enslaved was complicated by the dependence of the power-holders. In fact, plantation economies were famous for the extent of this dependence, the multiplicity of menial occupations, the overemployment of slave labor, and the languor and helplessness of the master class. Any careful reading of the history of a classic plantation colony—such as Jamaica, Saint-Domingue, or Suriname in the eighteenth century—reveals that the slaves must have known a good deal more about the intimate daily affairs of the masters than the masters could have known about those of the slaves. The relationships among the family members of the master were constantly monitored by domestic slaves of all kinds; and many white children in plantation colonies must have spent much more of their formative years in the company of their black governesses than in that of their mothers.

Yet a third type of contact was the sexual relationships between free and slave individuals. Expectably, such relationships usually involved slave women and free men. The contrary did occur, however, and careful study of the judicial records of almost any slave colony would probably uncover some cases of relationships between free women and slave men. For example, Van Lier, drawing on documents from Suriname, writes:

In 1711, two cases of sexual contact between a Negro and a white woman are reported, which prompted the promulgation by Governor Johan de Hoyer of an edict stipulating that a single white woman who had intercourse with a Negro was liable to a flogging and expulsion from the colony, while a married woman would be branded as well. Negroes were made liable to the death penalty for such an offense.

The immediate cause for the introduction of this legislation was a petition for divorce by a man by the name of Barend Roelofs, who stated "that his wife, Maria Keijser, having [had] carnal intimacy with a Negro and having become pregnant by him, had been delivered of a mulatto girl a few months previous." During the deliberations about this case the case of Judith de Castre, who had also had a child by a Negro but had since married a certain Jean Milton, also came up for discussion. The Hof [Court] resolved to have this Judith de Castre notified that neither she nor her mother, nor anyone else, no matter who, were ever to bring her mulatto child, or have it brought, to Paramaribo [the capital], on penalty of arbitrary punishment.[5]

For planters, it was crucial to deny that such relations could occur. It is interesting, when speculating about the frequency of such illicit unions, that both cases reported above involved pregnancies, and indeed births. It seems unlikely that, under other circumstances, they would have been made public at all.[6]

While many relationships involving sex between free and slave individuals were exploitative and often unspeakably cruel, others were marked by tenderness and esteem and endured in some cases for the lifetimes of the participants. Sexual contact between the free and the enslaved poses some of the most difficult and complex issues confronting the student of African-American history. On the one hand, such contacts could constitute the most serious threat of all—save revolution—to the plantation ideal. They were dangerous to the system not only because they spanned in a potentially compromising fashion the chasm between the slave and free sectors, but also because they resulted in children whose position was chronically ambiguous, even if legally they were slaves. On the other hand, paternity and the affective reality of the human relationships between slaves and masters in many cases complicated profoundly the ways in which the gulf between the powerful and the powerless was narrowed. Often, the European or Creole fathers of children born to slave women protected them, even if they did not (or legally could not) acknowledge them. In a relatively short period, the *affranchi* class of Saint-Domingue, for instance, consisting in large part of the children born to French masters by their female slaves, became economically and politically powerful in the colony.[7] While the picture is quite different in its ultimate consequences in a colony such as Jamaica, there, too, the same sexual bridging of the gap between the enslaved and free constituted a major point of contact between the two major sectors of the society.

Trade was another important area of contact. It is somewhat difficult to conceive of trade as an essential basis for encounter in a society where the majority of the population is enslaved, landless, and largely powerless. But the fact is that, in colony after colony, the slaves were forced (or permitted) to grow some part of their own subsistence. Repeatedly they became producers of a substantial portion of the total food consumed by the colony, including its free classes. Jamaica and Saint-Domingue once again provide a wealth of detail; the participation of the slaves in these two colonies was responsible for the growth of large and important markets in the towns and cities. Involved in such growth, moreover, was the acquisition by the slaves themselves of individual buying power, and an expansion of their consumption preferences. Numerous trading groups grew in the major centers of all the slave colonies, dependent upon the commerce of the slaves, and catering to their custom.

This list of occasions of contact can be easily lengthened: the role of slaves as musicians at European dances and festivals; as providers of special items for the delight of the master's family (such as fish and wild game); as ladies-in-waiting, chaperones, cicerones, and grooms.[8] The point, however, is that the slaves often found themselves playing an essentially instructional part with those who, within the system as such, held power over them. That the master class served both as teachers—and as intimidators—of the slaves, as regulators of their conduct, has always been matter of factly accepted and was doubtless usually true. But the role of the powerless in affecting and even controlling important parts of the lives of the masters was also typical of slave colonies and has not received enough attention.

We are building a schematic picture of societies deeply divided by status—and, accordingly, by physical type and much else—but complicated by the continuous interaction of members of both groups on many levels and in many different ways. We may view this schema first as consisting of the alignment of statuses and their accompanying roles: the dividing-up of tasks and responsibilities, of rights and obligations, in terms of power and authority. But we must also view it in terms of the ways cultural content—modes of behavior, styles of speech, beliefs and values, etiquette, cuisine, and the rest of the substance of daily conduct—was shaped, transmitted, and perpetuated. This change of focus enables us to see that the points of contact between persons of differing status, or different group membership, did not automatically determine the direction of flow of cultural materials according to the statuses of the participants, but according to other variables instead. The status of the master's child vis-à-vis his slave governess would surely affect his learning of a style of command in dealing with slaves. But his speech, his food preferences, his imagery, his earliest ideas about men and women, and a good deal more of what would become in time characteristic of him as an individual would be learned from someone far below him in status, but otherwise very much in control of him. Though this example may seem extreme, it is so only because we employ the image of infant and adult. We have no reason to suppose that it would be otherwise for the other areas of encounter between the enslaved and free, given this qualification. Although we choose not to pursue this part of the argument further here, any reflection upon the music, cuisine, folklore, dance, or speech of the American South ought to make it clear that it is anything but a perfect case of Europeans successfully "americanizing" their slaves, merely because they held a monopoly of power over them.

We may now specify some of the more obvious nodal points of contact and flow, recognizing that our list is only suggestive. To do so, we avoid the tendency to categorize culture in terms of major "topics" (economic, political, technological, folkloric, etc.), which rigidify somewhat the subject matter, choosing instead to think in terms of the interpersonal relationships through which cultural materials were mediated. One obvious relationship is that between free males and their paramours. An important aspect of these relationships would be the institutionalization of sexual attitudes among both the enslaved and the free concerning the sexuality of the opposing group. A second such relationship—or set of relationships—would be that between domestic slaves and those whom they tended: governess, cook, valet, and the members of the family resident in the so-called "great house" of the plantation. Of comparable importance would be the work relationships between the European staff and the "drivers," technicians, and foremen among the slaves. All these interactions were likely to be of long standing, and to be marked by at least some recognition of interdependence. To give only one example, the foods prepared by family cooks necessarily would involve some interchange of choices, shaped both by ancestral traditions and by the availability of foodstuffs. Just as it would be erroneous to assume that food preferences of the slaves were automatically predetermined by the prestige and power of the masters, it would be equally mistaken to suppose that European preferences alone would determine the cuisine that became conventional, choice, and "creole" over time. Lady Nugent's lively accounts, marked simultaneously by the ludicrous racism of a nineteenth-century New Jersey belle married to a Jamaican governor, and by endless assertions of her own humanitarianism, provide many examples of the extent to which the society of the Jamaican master class was informed by the culture of its slaves, even if this was not always acknowledged. Food is but one aspect of life in which this is brought firmly home.[9]

Many other examples from Lady Nugent's account reinforce our view of the flow of information and attitudes. For example, she describes a slave child who "could say the Lord's Prayer perfectly, but could not tell how she learnt it, both her father and mother are field negroes, and neither of them can say their prayers." At a later point she writes: "It is extraordinary to witness the immediate effect that the climate and habit of living in this country have upon the minds and manners of the Europeans, particularly of the lower orders. In the upper ranks, they become indolent and inactive regardless of everything but eating, drinking and indulging themselves, and are almost entirely under the dominion of their mulatto favorites. In the lower orders, they are the same, with the addition of conceit and tyranny." And finally, "The creole language is not confined to the negroes. Many of the ladies, who have not been educated in England, speak a sort of broken English, with an indolent drawling out of their words, that is very tiresome, if not disgusting. I stood next to a lady one night, near a window, and, by way of saying something, remarked that the air was much cooler than usual; to which she answered, 'Yes, ma'am, him rail-ly too fra-ish!' "[10] A number of authorities have dealt with many of these points, among them, and most eloquently, Edward Kamau Brathwaite.[11]

●

It has been our contention that the so-called creole cultures of the plantation colonies began to be forged during the earliest interaction of Europeans and Africans, and of Africans of different origins with each other, under conditions in which the outer parameters of variation were set by the environmental and ecological circumstances typical of subtropical colonies, by the overarching objectives of the plantation system, and by the monopoly of power vested in the European master classes. But we have stressed equally our view that the processes of culture formation were neither unilateral—the imposition of European forms upon passive African recipients—nor homogeneous. Rather, we feel that an adequate interpretation of these processes must begin with a careful examination of what is known about the points of contact between enslaved and free people, and the kinds of institutions (domestic, economic, religious, political) developed by each group to further its interests. In this section of the essay, we have emphasized the interactions between individuals drawn from each group, the kinds of materials that may have flowed from representatives of one group to representatives of the other, and the conventional points of contact, or "nodes," that emerged and crystallized within the existing social system. One final point perhaps deserves mention.

It is a social science commonplace that, in any social system, human interaction takes on its orderly character from the formalized expectations involved in playing out the roles attached to any particular status. In a slave society, of course, a central distinction arises from the legal differences between free persons and slaves. But such differences are reduced, magnified, and modulated variously, according to specific statuses within each sector, and according to the specific interactions between a free and an enslaved individual. In other words, the system of statuses neither fully expresses nor controls the range of possible specific interactions between individuals. This obvious but crucial aspect of social reality is expressed in whatever institution we examine in at least two significantly different regards. There are, firstly, cases of perceived "transgressions" that create acknowledged disturbance to the extent that they are public: adultery, cruelty to children, reneging on verbal agreements, various types of "insubordination," etc. Secondly, however, there is the implicitly (or even explicitly) acknowledged recognition of the range of variation typical of specific interactional settings, symbolized by a vocabulary of admiration or of reproval, as when terms such as "uppity," "nervy," "terribly polite," and "self-abasing" are employed to describe in greater detail an actual instance of encounter.

We believe this formulation must have been as true for the interaction in slave societies as it is for social life generally. However, interaction must have been complicated by the basic status-gap between the holders of power and those whom they controlled, but upon whom they were nonetheless deeply dependent. Such a system is expectably more rigid than one in which there is no such explicit and central division between two sectors. But this would not necessarily mean a smaller range of variation of behavior, so much as a heightened attention to the formal rules—the code—generated by a system designed for the inflexible control of one group by another. Whether one reads the account of an eighteenth-century observer of Jamaica or a novel by Faulkner, the emphasis on *form*, as opposed to the detail of content, is unmistakable. This emphasis expresses what we have in mind in speaking of the care required for effective role-playing in systems deeply cleft by a single primary criterion of status.

For slave societies in the New World, clearly standardized patterns of interaction between (free) whites and (enslaved) blacks must have been among the first kinds of social forms to become institutionalized. Such patterns probably solidified in an exaggerated fashion, because of the protection they offered against explicit violations, and because of the risks involved in a member of either group revealing to members of the other group his recognition of their humanity and individuality. Lady Nugent gives us yet another telling example:

As soon as that ceremony was over, I began the ball with an old Negro man. The gentlemen each selected a partner, according to rank, by age or service, and we all danced. However, I was not aware how much I shocked the Misses Murphy by doing this; for I did exactly the same as I would have done at a servants' hall birth-day in England. They told me, afterwards, that they were nearly fainting, and could hardly forbear shedding a flood of tears, at such an unusual and extraordinary sight; for in this country, and among slaves, it was necessary to keep up so much more distant respect! They may be right. I meant nothing wrong, and all the poor creatures seemed so delighted, and so much pleased, that I could scarcely repent it. I was, nevertheless, very sorry to have hurt their feelings, and particularly too as they seemed to think the example dangerous, as making the blacks of too much consequence, or putting them all on a footing with the whites, they said, might produce a serious change in their conduct, and even produce a rebellion in the Island.[12]

What we have sought finally to stress in this section is that the presence of this carefully defined code of behavior emphatically does not mean that all such instances of interaction were void of either humanity or individual variation—in fact, quite the contrary.[13]

3

THE SLAVE SECTOR

~~~~~~

For most of the social relationships in which the slaves were involved, the society of free people was tangential or peripheral—for slave life remained in many ways disengaged from the concerns of the masters. This may seem a paradoxical or contradictory assertion in view of the preceding discussion. But we must draw our distinctions between the slave and free groups carefully. That they were usually locked into an intimate interdependence is, in our view, inarguable. But we have sought to stress the often quite striking incomprehension of the true nature of this interdependence on the part of the masters, as well as their lack of awareness of the extent to which their own lives and attitudes were shaped by a slave-based economy and by the behaviors of the slaves themselves. We are not as certain—in fact, we doubt very much—that the slaves were similarly uncomprehending. In any case, a good deal of the interaction between members of these two sectors must have taken place according to conventionalized expectations that concealed as much as they revealed about each group. So far as the slaves' ways of life are concerned, we suspect that, in many areas, it was the masters' control that mattered most, by imposing outside limits on innovative adaptation.

Phillippo recounts the story of a Jamaican slave caught stealing sugar, who denied repeatedly that he stole, insisting that he had only "taken" the sugar: " 'As sugar belongs to massa, and myself belongs to massa, it all de same ting—dat make me tell massa me don't tief; me only take it!' 'What do you call thieving, then?' 'When me broke into broder house and ground, and take away him ting, den me tief, massa.' "[1] More striking yet is Phillippo's story of the slave mother who beats her child for telling an overseer where a fugitive slave had run: "Next time buckra ax you which side neger run, you tell him me no know, massa." As Phillippo puts it, somewhat exasperatedly, "Truth, indeed, was designated in negro parlance 'telling lies to buckra.' "[2] And other narrative materials document richly the precise ways in which the slave and free sectors remained at once profoundly intertwined yet clearly separate.

We would contend, then, that the institutions created by the slaves to deal with what are at once the most ordinary and most important aspects of life took on their characteristic shape *within* the parameters of the masters' monopoly of power, but *separate from* the masters' institutions.[3] We have in mind, for example, how slaves mended their clothes, furnished their houses, cooked their meals, fell in love, courted, married, bore and socialized their children, worshipped their deities, organized their "plays" and other recreation, and buried their dead. If our assertions in this regard are interpreted too literally, of course, we can easily be proved wrong; in theory, the masters could determine how all of these activities were organized,

given their power and its exercise. Yet we have many dem-
onstrations of the way the masters came to accept the pattern-
ings of slave institutions as part of daily reality and to which
they, too, had to adjust.[4] It is not a particularly sophisticated
assertion that enslavement involved the masters, as well as the
slaves, in patterned behaviors. We would add to this assertion
no more than that slave institutions and the life of the slaves
need to be analyzed as much as possible in light of this fact.

The nodal or core institutions around which slaves ordered
their lives would be concerned with such basic problems as
establishing friendships, evolving kin groups, constituting domestic units, perfecting life-crisis solutions (the social pattern-
ing to handle birth, illness, death), establishing religious
groups, and solving the problems of servility (by dissimulation,
malingering, etc.). Here, we engage the problem of how such
heterogeneous aggregates of men and women could compose
a social order for themselves, within the boundaries of ma-
neuver defined by the masters' monopoly of power. In attempting to put our emphasis upon the social-relational
problems that faced the slaves, we do not intend to ignore or
to deemphasize the cultural materials that would inform their
nascent institutions. But these cultural materials, we submit,
are best seen as an aspect of the growth of institutions, the
persons involved, and the sorts of coherence they must have
come to provide to the slave community as a whole.

The growth of institutions patterned for the total slave complement of a plantation would give coherence to the slave
community, but a coherence inevitably complicated by ex-
pectable divisions or differences. Births and deaths, problems
of love and hate, the introduction of new cargoes of the enslaved into a community already functioning, the sale of members and the forced fragmentation of families or domestic

groups—these and many other influences would affect the kind and degree of coherence a slave community might achieve. Once effective slave institutions became operative among a miscellaneous aggregate of slaves, that aggregate, in turn, would begin to become a community. Thereupon the more divisive or disruptive aspects of life could begin to work themselves out against an existing structure of behavioral patterns, as happens in any social system.

The institutions that emerged in any early slave population may be viewed as a sort of framework in which cultural materials could be employed, standardized, and transformed into new tradition. Thus, whether we have in mind the way slaves fell in love and created familial groupings, or the way they gathered in regular groupings to worship, the content of such behavior can be viewed as an aspect of the social relationships. Such a view puts a very different light, we think, on any reflection about "africanisms." It should no longer seem sufficient to maintain that Haiti's twin cult, the worship of Shango (Xango) in Trinidad or Bahia, or the use of oracles in Suriname are simply examples of Africa transplanted, or even of specific ethnic continuities of culture. Our task must rather be to delineate the processes by which those cultural materials that were retained could contribute to the institution-building the slaves undertook to inform their condition with coherence, meaning, and some measure of autonomy.

4

THE BEGINNINGS OF AFRICAN-AMERICAN SOCIETIES AND CULTURES

~~~~~

Before any aggregate of plantation slaves could begin to create viable institutions, they would have had to deal with the traumata of capture, enslavement, and transport. Hence the beginnings of what would later develop into "African-American cultures" must date from the very earliest interactions of the newly enslaved men and women on the African continent itself. They were shackled together in the coffles, packed into dank "factory" dungeons, squeezed together between the decks of stinking ships, separated often from their kinsmen, tribesmen, or even speakers of the same language, left bewildered about their present and their future, stripped of all prerogatives of status or rank (at least, so far as the masters were concerned), and homogenized by a dehumanizing system that viewed them as faceless and largely interchangeable. Yet we know that even in such utterly abject circumstances, these people were not simply passive victims. In the present context, we are thinking less of the many individual acts of heroism and resistance which occurred during this period than of certain simple but significant *cooperative* efforts which, in retrospect, may be viewed as the true beginnings of African-American culture and society.

Various shreds of evidence suggest that some of the earliest social bonds to develop in the coffles, in the factories and, especially, during the long Middle Passage were of a dyadic (two-person) nature. Partly, perhaps, because of the general policy of keeping men and women separate, they were usually between members of the same sex. The bond between ship-mates, those who shared passage on the same slaver, is the most striking example. In widely scattered parts of Afro-America, the "shipmate" relationship became a major principle of social organization and continued for decades or even centuries to shape ongoing social relations.

In Jamaica, for example, we know that the term "shipmate" was "synonymous in their [the slaves'] view with 'brother' or 'sister.' "[1] It was "the dearest word and bond of affectionate sympathy amongst the Africans," and "so strong were the bonds between shipmates that sexual intercourse between them, in the view of one observer, was considered incestuous."[2] We know also that the bond could extend beyond the original shipmates themselves and interpenetrate with biological kin ties; shipmates were said to "look upon each other's children mutually as their own," and "it was customary for children to call their parents' shipmates 'uncle' and 'aunt.' "[3]

In Suriname, to cite a different case, the equivalent term "sippi" was at first used between people who had actually shared the experience of transport in a single vessel; later, it began to be used between slaves who belonged to a single plantation, preserving the essential notion of fellow sufferers who have a special bond.[4] Today in the interior of Suriname, among the Saramaka people, "sippi" (now "sibi") continues to designate a special, nonbiological dyadic relationship with very similar symbolic content; when two people find themselves victims of a parallel misfortune (e.g., two women whose husbands desert them at about the same time), they thenceforth may address each other as "sibi" and adopt a special prescribed mutual relationship.

Other examples of the "shipmate" relationship in Afro-America can be cited—from the Brazilian "malungo"[5] and Trinidadian "malongue"[6] to Suriname "máti"[7] to Haitian "batiment."[8] But we have said enough already to support the following assertions. It is not surprising that same-sex dyadic ties should have loomed large in the earliest context of African-American enslavement and transport (given that such ties seem often to develop when random individuals are thrust into an institutional, depersonalized setting—such as boot camp or prison). What may make this case unusual is the extent to which such initial bonds could develop into basic principles which probably helped to shape the institutions of such societies and which, even today, in many areas appear to retain their original symbolic content. We believe that the development of these social bonds, even before the Africans had set foot in the New World, already announced the birth of new societies based on new kinds of principles.

Our argument proceeds here in the light of our earlier discussions concerning the concept of a generalized African "heritage" and the distinction between cultural and social-relational perspectives in Afro-Americanist research. Just as the development of new social ties marked the initial enslavement experience, so also new *cultural systems* were beginning to take shape. We shall speculate on some of the processes that must have been involved in the earliest growth of African-American religions, drawing upon our understanding that, in religion as in many other West and Central African cultural subsystems, an apparent diversity of form fits with certain widely shared basic principles. As in our previous discussion, we seek to conceptualize these principles without reference to specific, overt manifestations. Thus, for instance, most West and Central African religions seem to have shared certain fundamental assumptions about the nature of causality and the ability of divination to reveal specific causes, about the active role of the dead in the lives of the living, about the responsiveness of (most) deities to human actions, about the close relationship between social conflict and illness or misfortune, and many others.[9] Moreover, ritual knowledge in these societies tended to be specialized and "owned" by individuals or cult groups, and such knowledge was transmitted either along genealogical lines or via initiation into a cult group. Since so much of West and Central African religion was instrumental in orientation (or at least focused on specific, special events, from illnesses to coronations), the proportion of substantive ritual knowledge that was in the hands of specialists was considerable. We would suggest also that this instrumental orientation of ritual encouraged experimentation with, and adoption of, new techniques and practices from neighboring peoples; we suspect that most West and Central African religions were relatively permeable to foreign influences and tended to be "additive" rather than "exclusive" in their orientation toward other cultures.

These generalities may help us to imagine something of the initial cultural situation for an aggregate of recently enslaved Africans. We can probably date the beginnings of any new African-American religion from the moment that one person in need received ritual assistance from another who belonged to a different cultural group. Once such people had "exchanged" ritual assistance in this fashion, there would already exist a micro-community with a nascent religion that was, in a real sense, its own. We may speculate, for example, that one of the earliest slaves on a particular plantation in a new colony gives birth to twins (or becomes insane, commits suicide, or has any one of a number of experiences which would have required *some* kind of highly specialized ritual attention in almost any society in West or Central Africa). It is clear to all that *something* must be done, but our hypothetical mother of twins has no special expertise herself, nor does anyone of her own ethnic background on that plantation. However, another woman, one of whose relatives may have been a priestess of a twin cult in another group, takes charge of the situation, performing the rites as best she can remember them. By dint of this experience, then, this woman becomes *the* local specialist in twin births. In caring ritually for their parents, in performing the special rites necessary should they sicken or die, and so on, she may eventually transmit her specialized knowledge (which may well be a fairly radical selection and elaboration of what her relative's cult had been) to other slaves, who thereupon carry this knowledge, and the attached statuses and roles, forward in time.

This speculative exercise requires that we notice the probable openness of such situations to the introduction of new cultural materials, as well as the way new ritual formulations become attached to an institutional structure, in the form of specialized personnel. During even a short period of time, exchanges of ritual information among those who shared certain underlying assumptions would have contributed importantly to the formation of integrated cultural subsystems. The initial cultural heterogeneity of the enslaved doubtless had the effect of forcing them at the outset to shift their primary cultural and social commitment from the Old World to the New, a process which often took their European masters centuries to accomplish.[10] The quite radical cultural reorientation that must have typified the adaptation of enslaved Africans to the New World was surely more extreme than what the European colonists—with their more intact institutions, continuing contacts with the homeland, and more coherent family groupings—experienced. Even in those special situations in which some members of a particular ethnic or linguistic group could remain in close contact, such orientation must have remained a secondary focus of commitment, with the new African-American culture and its concomitant social ties being primary. All slaves must have found themselves accepting, albeit out of necessity, countless "foreign" cultural practices, and this implied a gradual remodeling of their own traditional ways of doing many things. For most individuals, a commitment to, and engagement in, a new social and cultural world must have taken precedence rather quickly over what would have become before long largely a nostalgia for their homelands. We remind ourselves and our readers that people ordinarily do not long for a lost "cultural heritage" in the abstract, but for the immediately experienced personal relationships, developed in a specific cultural and institutional setting, that any trauma such as war or enslavement may destroy. A "culture," in these terms, becomes intimately linked to the social contexts within which affective ties are experienced and perceived. With the destruction of those ties, each individual's "cultural set" is transformed phenomenologically, until the creation of new institutional frameworks permits the refabrication of content, both based upon—and much removed from—the past.

We have been suggesting that distinctive, "mature" African-American cultures and societies probably developed more rapidly than has often been assumed. The early forging of "shipmate" ties or ritual complexes, as we have phrased them, are intended as arbitrary (though central) examples of much more general processes. Even in the realm of the arts, to choose a less likely example, it could be shown that new cultural subsystems were worked out through the interaction of slaves who had not yet set foot in the Americas. Not only was drumming, dancing, and singing encouraged for "exercise" on many of the slavers,[11] but Stedman tells us how, at the end of the nightmare of the Middle Passage, off the shores of Suriname: "All the Slaves are led upon deck . . . their hair shaved in different figures of Stars. half-moons, &c, /which they generally do the one to the other (having no Razors) by the help of a broken bottle and without Soap/."[12] It is hard to imagine a more impressive example of irrepressible cultural vitality than this image of slaves decorating one another's hair in the midst of one of the most dehumanizing experiences in all of history.

To document our assertions that fully formed African-American cultures developed within the earliest years of settlement in many New World colonies involves genuine difficulties. These stem from the general shortage of descriptive materials on slave life during the initial period, as well as from the lack of research regarding this problem. However, in at least one colony—Suriname—certain fortuitous historical events allow us to pinpoint in time the development of several major cultural subsystems, and we are able to find support for our broader argument.

Language provides one relevant case. Within the first twenty years of settlement, almost all of the English planters who had established the colony of Suriname left for other parts of the

Caribbean, taking their slaves with them. During the several years when the newly imported, Dutch-owned slaves over-lapped with the soon to depart English-owned slaves, the language developed by the English-owned slaves must have been passed on to these new arrivals. This, at least, is our conclusion, because ever since that time, three hundred years ago, an English-based creole (called Sranan, Negro-English, Surinaams, or Taki-Taki) has been the national language of Suriname. This language, a new African-American creation, can reliably be said to have been "firmly established" within the colony's first two decades.[13]

The rapidity with which a complex, integrated, and unique African-American religious system developed in Suriname at a very early point is no less striking. Our evidence, again, is indirect but quite suggestive. When the ancestors of the Saramaka Maroons escaped from the plantations of the Para and the Lower Suriname Rivers to establish an independent society in the forested interior (during the seventeenth and very early eighteenth centuries), they must have carried with them a religious system that had already been rather fully shaped on the plantations. There are remarkable similarities today between the religious systems of the Saramaka and of the "Creoles" of the Para region, similarities which range from countless specific belief-rite complexes, such as that surrounding the killing of a tapir, to broad-based principles like those relating corporate groups and their ancestral gods; these similarities cannot be explained adequately on the basis of subsequent contact.[14] Moreover, today—now that there is freedom of movement for Saramakas going to the coast—a specific group of Saramakas will commonly visit, worship, and exchange specialized ritual information with those "Creoles" who are precisely the descendants of slaves who lived on the same plantation from which the ancestors of that particular group of Saramakas had fled, over two and one-half centuries ago.

We can assert with some confidence, then, that during the earliest decades of the African presence in Suriname, the core of a new language and a new religion had been developed; subsequent centuries of massive new importations from Africa apparently had little more effect than to lead to secondary elaborations. We would suggest tentatively that similar scenarios may have unfolded in many other parts of Afro-America, and for other cultural sub-systems as well. Handler and Frisbie, for example, appear to argue similarly in dealing with music among Barbadian slaves.[15]

However, we do not mean to imply that in some special situations, late-arriving Africans were not able to exert considerable influence on local African-American institutions (see below). Rather, the Suriname data simply suggest to us the need for considerably more detailed research on such problems. When we can chart the growth of African-American social and cultural systems in a fairly precise time perspective, we will be able to consider, for example, the relationship between the provenience of the mass of Africans and the cultural forms developing in a given colony at a particular time, and we will have taken a large step toward understanding how African-American cultures were actually forged.

We have stressed some of the ways in which the early stages of African-American history fostered the rapid development of local slave cultures. But we believe that this distinctive setting also stamped these cultures with certain general features that strongly influenced their subsequent development and continue to lend to them much of their characteristic shape today. Our speculation runs as follows. While the greatest shock of enslavement was probably the fear of physical violence and of death itself, the psychological accompaniment of this trauma was the relentless assault on personal identity, being stripped of status and rank and treated as nameless ciphers. Yet, by a peculiar irony, this most degrading of all aspects of slavery seems to have had the effect of encouraging the slaves to cultivate an enhanced appreciation for exactly those most personal, most human characteristics which differentiate one individual from another, perhaps the principal qualities which the masters could not take away from them. Early on, then, the slaves were elaborating upon the ways in which they could be individuals—a particular sense of humor, a certain skill or type of knowledge, even a distinctive way of walking or talking, or some sartorial detail, like the cock of a hat or the use of a cane.

At the same time, as we have seen, the initial cultural heterogeneity of the enslaved produced among them a general openness to ideas and usages from other cultural traditions, a special tolerance (within the West African context) of cultural differences. We would suggest that this acceptance of cultural differences combined with the stress on personal style to produce in early African-American cultures a fundamental dynamism, an expectation of cultural change as an integral feature of these systems. Within the strict limits set by the conditions of slavery, African-Americans learned to put a premium on innovation and individual creativity; there was always a place for fads and fashions; "something new" (within certain aesthetic limits, of course) became something to be celebrated, copied, and elaborated; and a stylistic innovation brought by a newly imported African could be quickly assimilated. From the first, then, the commitment to a new culture by African-Americans in a given place included an expectation of continued dynamism, change, elaboration, and creativity.[16]

5
RETENTIONS AND SURVIVALS

~~~~~~

If African-American cultures do in fact share such an integral dynamism, and if, as we shall argue, their social systems have been highly responsive to changing social conditions, one must maintain a skeptical attitude toward claims that many contemporary social or cultural forms represent direct continuities from the African homelands. Over the past several decades, historical research has reduced the number of convincing cases of formal continuities, but has hinted at new levels of continuity—levels which may eventually tell us a great deal more about the actual development of African-American cultures. Students of the African-American heritage have witnessed a gradual shift from the analysis of isolated cultural elements viewed largely from the outside, to the analysis of systems or patterns in their social context. Students of creole languages, for example, increasingly have located the unique aspects of these languages on the syntactic (or discourse) level, rather than simply on the lexical level; and analogous arguments have

been proposed for such diverse things as art forms and onomastics.[1]

These shifting perspectives are well illustrated by the history
of studies of Suriname Maroon woodcarving. Traditionally,
scholars considered this to be the prototypical "African art in
the Americas";[2] an art historian discussing this art among the
Saramaka has noted that the "arabesques in open-
work . . . even-sided flat bands, and . . . brass studs to enhance curvilinearity" strikingly recall eighteenth-century Akan
work.[3] Yet recent ethnohistorical field research strongly suggests that this distinctive art form was forged in the Guianas
and is largely a nineteenth-century development. It has also
demonstrated that many of the most striking formal similarities
with West African art are quite recent innovations.[4] More
generally, such research urges upon us a reorientation of our
focus, from trying to explain similarities of form considered
in isolation to comparing broad aesthetic ideas, the implicit
"grammatical" principles which generate these forms. The very
real formal similarities between the art of the Maroons and
that of some West African peoples are not, then, mere evidence
of static "retentions" or "survivals," but rather products of
independent development and innovation, within historically
related and overlapping sets of broad aesthetic ideas. The woodcarving of the Maroons, like their naming, cicatrization, and
other aesthetic systems, then appears to be highly creative and
to be "African" more in terms of deep-level cultural rules or
principles than in terms of formal continuities: in short, a
highly adaptive subsystem, responsive to the changing social
environments of the artists and critics who continue to carry
it forward.

We keep in mind that, in art as in much else, the relationships between individual artist and group are likely to be complex and subtle. To what extent art is produced and modified in a context of freedom of expression, and to what extent group and individual creator are bound by conservative values, must be specified separately for each society and, often, for each art medium or genre. We can assume that West African artistic expression varied to some degree from one society to another, while the opportunity for individual creativeness or innovativeness probably varied with the social function of the particular art form. Presumably much the same has been the case with African-American art. Given the social circumstances of its beginnings, however, we choose to suppose that a high degree of freedom for variation may have been institutionalized in many art forms at the outset. In order to make the most possible sense of how these forms evolved in African-American societies, it will be necessary both to learn all we can of those initial situations, and to pursue our study of art and other African-American cultural manifestations in their social contexts,[5] and not purely as delineations of changing or conservative forms.

Recent historical research on Afro-America also has taught us some of the dangers of extrapolating backward to Africa in the realm of *social* forms. We may mention but one obvious example drawn from our own work. Saramaka men, who now commonly have two wives each, turn out upon careful investigation to be far more "polygynous" (one might say "African-looking," in Herskovits's terms) today than were their ancestors two centuries ago, due to changing institutions in the wider society, with newly evolved patterns of wage labor and the skewed local sex ratios such patterns have created.[6] It seems likely that systems of social relations are generally even more highly responsive to changing environmental conditions than are cultural systems. As in the cultural realm, however, we would suggest that delving below the surface of social forms to get at the value systems and cognitive orientations that underlie and accompany them may reveal long-term continuities of another kind.

In calling for more subtle, in-depth research, we do not mean to deny the existence of direct "survivals" or "retentions" in Afro-America, or that careful investigation of the specific reasons for their continued persistence will help us better to understand the formative years of African-American history. We might cite two brief examples. The ultimate "ordeal," the equivalent of the highest court in Saramaka today, is in the hands of a small cult group in a single village; its techniques, which include thrusting a medicated feather through the tongue of the accused to determine guilt or innocence, seem traceable directly to the eighteenth-century Kingdom of Benin.[7] In this case, it seems likely that a specific cluster of ritual knowledge was carried to Suriname during the earliest years of slavery by a single specialist, and that the tradition (which is attested to in eighteenth-century Saramaka[8]) was perpetuated in much the same way as we describe for our hypothetical "twin birth" ritual. In contrast, divination with a coffin—the interrogation of the spirit of the deceased (in which the movements of the bearers of the corpse are "controlled" by the spirit, anxious to reveal the cause of death)— provides a different sort of example. It was a widespread practice in West and Central Africa as part of funeral rites, and we find it again in widely separated parts of colonial Afro-America—from Jamaica to Dominica to Suriname.[9] Unlike the Saramaka ordeal, which involves a highly specialized body of knowledge from a particular society that nevertheless served a function recognized as crucial in many West and Central

African societies, divination with the corpse was probably familiar to most of the first transported slaves. These two particular continuities, even viewed thus summarily, can be seen to illustrate somewhat different processes in the development of African-American cultures. Careful consideration of other such real historical continuities almost certainly will help us to understand some of the choices open to early African-Americans, as well as the later course their cultures took.

We wish to consider, in equally sketchy fashion, two other cases of continuity, partly in order to emphasize the relationship between continuity of culture and continuity of personnel, partly to enlarge the range of cases of such continuities, and to expose the complexity involved in their study. Following Emancipation in the British West Indies (1834–1838), free Africans were imported to a number of British colonies, including Trinidad, in the hope of expanding agricultural settlement and of supplying additional labor to the planters. In a twenty-year period (1841–1861), Trinidad received 6,581 *free* Africans;[10] between 1834 and 1867, that island received a total of 8,854 *liberated* Africans, taken off slavers headed for Cuba or Brazil by British cruisers.[11] A large number of different African cultural groups were represented by these migrations, including Ibo, Temne, Wolof, Yoruba, Ashanti, Fulani, and Mandingo peoples.[12]

In a tantalizingly brief but intriguing account, Carr described a "rada" (Dahomean) community outside Port-of-Spain, founded by one Robert Antoine (Aboyevi Zāhwenu) about fifteen years after his arrival in Trinidad. Antoine acquired a small property by purchase in 1868, where he settled with his common-law wife and son. By the time of his death in 1899, his house and compound had become a center for migrant Dahomeans, many of whom had previously settled nearby: "during the ceremonial occasions of those early days it is said that so large were the gatherings at the compound that there was hardly room in which to accommodate the people."[13]

Antoine initiated and maintained a substantial portion of the Dahomean ceremonial calendar at his compound. It is significant that those who emigrated at the same time to Trinidad had included a trained *hubonō* or high priest, and two male *vodūnsi* (cult initiates), and all three of these men actively perpetuated traditional ceremonies. It may be of equal interest that the gods who are celebrated by this group often carry saints' names, typical of African-American religious groupings in Catholic countries elsewhere, as in Brazil, Cuba, and Haiti. Carr asked his informants how the African deities acquired Christian names and was told that they had "always" had them. The idea that such names had been attached to the African godheads after contact with missionaries in Africa was rejected by the elderly compound member with whom Carr spoke. Thus we have no information as to how or when such names were in fact acquired.

It is not our intent here to examine in detail the correspondences and divergences between the religious expressions of this group and those typical of nineteenth-century Dahomey. But we must note that this case reveals both substantial continuity—as in calendrical allocation of ceremonies, gods' names, priestly roles, sacrifice, possession, etc.—and substantial modification, both by syncretism (for instance, the attachment of saints' names, which we believe to have occurred in Trinidad itself) and in terms of the sociology of the new setting. No male *vodūnsis* have appeared since the deaths of Alokasu and Kunu, who accompanied Antoine from Africa. The *Kututɔ* ceremony for the dead, which is held in November, is now linked to a Catholic mass for the souls in Purgatory. Five deities, who formerly possessed native African migrants, have not reappeared since the deaths of these men. Some shrines have vanished. Even in small ways, change reveals itself. The *Sakpata* shrine, still maintained in the compound, once had at its head a euphorbia plant, supposedly in accord with African tradition. But a child's eyesight was damaged by the milky fluid of the plant some years ago, whereupon it was replaced with a dragonblood plant (*Dracaena* spp.).

Even without a thorough comparative examination, it should be clear that the sociocultural religious system of the homeland did not survive intact and unchanged in the new context—and, of course, it would be quite extraordinary if it had. Doubtless more significant is the fact that Antoine was able to count on the services of three trained religious specialists when he initiated the ceremonial calendar a century ago. While we cannot weigh the importance of the disappearance of male *vodūnsis*, we think it defensible to assume that it would have affected the forms and functions of the ceremonial calendar today.

A final example may be drawn from the literature on Afro-Cuban religion. While it differs in many ways from that provided above, it shares with the Trinidadian case a relative recency of implantation of African custom in the New World setting. The slave trade to Cuba ended about 1865, though it seems certain that additional slaves were imported during several years immediately following. Curtin has estimated that twelve thousand slaves were imported in 1865, but calls this "guesswork," and suggests that he has picked a relatively high figure because he supposes that the trade continued briefly thereafter.[14] Materials on the ethnic origins of Cuban slaves during the last stages of the trade are unsatisfactory; the trade was illegal, and manifests of slave ships, or other information of the sort available for, say, Saint-Domingue at an earlier period, are lacking. Nonetheless, it is certain that substantial numbers of Yoruba were imported, and the Afro-Cuban religious and linguistic materials suggest as much. Having carried out field investigations both among the Yoruba of Ife, Nigeria, and the Lucumí of Matanzas, Cuba, Bascom and Montero de Bascom were able to document continuities of certain kinds in divinatory practices, including the 256 permutations resulting from the casting of a sixteen-unit, two-part divinatory necklace. Though important changes in the materials employed, in the terminology of explanation, and in the pronunciation of terms have occurred, "Both the names and the order of the double figures . . . check exactly with those recorded for the Yoruba by Epega, Aderoju, Frobenius, Monteil, and Dennett, for Dahomey by Bertho and Maupoil, and for the Ewe by Spieth."[15] The Afro-Cuban data are particularly convincing because the various elements in divinatory practices are clearly separable, but occur in both Nigeria and Cuba in such intimate interrelationship that diffusion from Africa to the New World cannot be questioned seriously.

These two cases reveal both continuity and change. The Afro-Cuban case makes clear that a relatively complex portion of culture can be carried substantially intact from one locus to another. Though certain substitutions of material (e.g. coconut disks for kola nuts) occur and are obvious enough, migrant diviners needed only to have around them persons from the same or a related society where such divination was practiced to have been able to ply their skills. The Afro-Cuban divinatory practices, however, both show continuities with more than one West African culture and suggest that other groups besides the Yoruba contributed to the forms assumed by older materials in the Cuban context. The Trinidadian case does not demonstrate any obvious intermixture of original African forms, even though there was considerable change in the new setting over time. The Cuban case suggests that the African materials diffused from overseas originated with persons who were members of different groups, even though very solid continuities with past practice are demonstrable.

Two obvious features of these cases require mention. First, both of the emigrations in question, relative to certain others, occurred fairly recently. Second, in one case the migrants were free or freedmen, and, in the other, slavery had ended only about twenty-five years after the last migration. In both of these regards, the Trinidadian and Cuban examples differ substantially from most other examples of African continuities. In a general way, it can be claimed that both the strength of the continuities and their relative lack of modification probably are related to recency of migration and to the presence (in Trinidad) or nearness (in Cuba) of freedom. Such assertions do not explain away the many other cases of such continuities, often maintained in the face of great oppression and imposed disorder, nor can we deal adequately here with the whole issue of illegal slave trading, as it must have influenced the whole panorama of continuities in the New World. But overall, direct formal continuities from Africa are more the exception than the rule in any African-American culture, even in those such as Saramaka, which have been most isolated.[16]

6
KINSHIP AND SEX ROLES

~~~~~~~~

We have been suggesting that a firm grounding in what is known of the past of African-American peoples can enhance our understanding of their present, much as the study of the present provides clues that can be carried fruitfully into archival research. Some additional emphasis on the uses of the past is called for, certainly not to the exclusion of ethnography, but as an essential corollary, particularly in the case of African-American cultures. Given the tension-ridden initial situations in which enslaved Africans found themselves, we believe that one promising strategy—though by no means the only one—for plotting the rise of African-American cultures would be to focus on the beginnings, from which we can work forward, rather than simply to extrapolate backward on the basis of perceived similarities with Old World cultures.

If we force ourselves to consider in all its complexity the initial situation of Africans in any New World colony, few of the "historical" explanations offered by scholars for current African-American cultural or social forms are likely to turn out to be fully adequate. In exploring the choices people actually faced during the formative years of these cultures, a broad range of variables must be taken into account, from ethnic composition of the slave masses or the specific and highly differentiated social conditions in a particular colony at a given time, to the geographical distribution in Africa of particular beliefs and practices. In terms of our current knowledge, it seems reasonable to expect that almost any subsystem of an African-American culture—whether music, speech, or religion—would be highly syncretistic in terms of its diverse African origins, as well as in terms of inputs from European (and often other) sources; and we must expect it to possess a built-in internal dynamism and a marked adaptiveness to changing social conditions as well. This implies that the task of reconstructing the history of any such system or institutional complex is immensely challenging but fraught with pitfalls.

With all this in mind, we nevertheless would like to sketch in a partial outline of such an enterprise. It may help to bring some of our programmatic generalities to life and even, perhaps, to point to some promising lines of future inquiry.

For many years, the controversy about the proper theories and methods to be used in the study of African-American culture history centered on "the Negro family," and much of this debate is probably familiar to the reader. It may be useful, therefore, to focus on this particular institutional complex, in order to highlight the concepts that may distinguish our general approach from more traditional conceptualizations.

Melville J. Herskovits and E. Franklin Frazier were the major protagonists in the ongoing "debate" over the black family, each calling upon history in the effort to explain current social forms, but with very different ideas about the nature of the African-American historical experience.[1] Herskovits, who tended to treat social structure as an aspect of "culture," stressed the ultimate African origin of New World family forms. Discussing Haiti, for example, he asserted that "the institution of plural marriage . . . is obviously African"; in Trinidadian marriage forms, he saw "a translation [reinterpretation], in terms of the monogamic pattern of European mating, of basic West African forms that operate within a polygynous frame."[2] Numerous similar statements could be cited.

Frazier, in contrast, viewed the African-American past in terms of its relevance for the understanding of contemporary institutions, as beginning only with the process of enslavement and transport. In one of his most forceful statements on the matter, he wrote that "probably never before in history has a people been so nearly stripped of its social heritage as were the Negroes who were brought to America"; and he argued that images of the African past were merely "Forgotten Memories."[3] For Frazier, African-Americans were culturally deprived, frustrated Americans; and another sociologist, applying Frazier's ideas to the Jamaican slave, would conclude that his "ideals and attitudes and morals and manners were more or less those of his masters."[4] Whether in the United States or in Jamaica, if the institutions of African-Americans were not identical to those of the American mainstream, it was, according to this view, only because of a long and terrible history of oppression.[5]

Though such a thumbnail sketch of the Herskovits-Frazier positions may overstate the contrast between these views of African-Americans, the contrast is no less real. In one view, African-Americans were essentially Africans, whose commitments to their ancestral past made them culturally different from other Americans; in the other view, they were merely Americans who had not been able to acculturate fully because of their oppression. Clearly, this controversy is far from dead, and a great deal of argument continues as to whether African-Americans have a different culture or different cultures, or are simply the victims of deprivation. Yet the polemical nature of these arguments, as well as their strongly political flavor, has led many Caribbeanists to reject out of hand historical considerations in analyzing family institutions. One such authority claims that historical approaches "only seek to explain the existence of Caribbean family systems as a general type," and another that "historical, cultural, structural, and psychological theories developed with such care to 'explain' the peculiar Caribbean family system are primarily of value as items in the history of social thought."[6] Though we might seek to explain what led these anthropologists to an ahistorical position, that is not our purpose here. Instead, we intend once again, in the discussion which follows, to argue the very real need for historical research for an understanding of the family or, for that matter, of any other African-American institution.

One of our major postulates has been that neither social context nor cultural traditions alone can explain an African-American institutional form[7] and that the development of institutions must be viewed in their full historical setting. In terms of the family, any number of simple illustrations come to mind. In one Martiniquan fishing village, for instance, current contrasts in family form (e.g., differing frequencies of female-headed households or of marital stability) are related directly to differing historical experiences. The residents at one end of the village are descended from people who abandoned plantation life only four generations ago, and the relatively "loose" institutional complex (with its associated values) relating to "the family" on plantations continues to influence them today. In contrast, the inhabitants of the other end of the village have a long heritage as independent fishermen on this site, dating back to pre-Emancipation times, and their more stable family forms can be directly related to this fact.[8] This argument, of course, is not restricted to African-Americans.[9] To explain family forms among East Indian estate workers in Guyana, for example, one could hardly proceed without taking into account both cultural traditions and social conditions. As one student of these people has noted, their families are, in general, much less "matricentric" than one would expect, given their socioeconomic situation (and keeping local African-American patterns in mind), yet much more so than one would predict on the basis of their attitudes or values. Jayawardena has shown that variations in family form among local East Indian villages can be fully understood only by examining the particular ways people turned their cultural resources to the task of adapting to new and varied social environments.[10]

One of the problems with many traditional studies of the black family—and this applies to those of Herskovits as well as to those of Frazier—was a tendency to reify the concept of "family" itself. Though anthropologists, at considerable cost, finally have learned otherwise, many historians may not yet be aware of the implications of such reification. For example, in Afro-America the "household" unit need by no means correspond to "the family," however defined. It is, for example, common for domestic groups (those which pool economic resources, share responsibility for socializing children, etc.) to span several households; for the composition of a household to be determined by factors other than kinship; and so on. In studying family institutions, then, a number of distinctions should be drawn between those ideas and practices relating to kinship, those relating to mating or marriage, those relating to residence and household, and those relating to the allocation of domestic responsibilities.[11] The development of kinship and sex roles among African-Americans will be used to illustrate the necessity for such distinctions, and also to point up the complexities involved in tracing the growth of any African-American institution.

Let us begin, once again, with a hypothetical aggregate of recently enslaved Africans on a new plantation in the Americas. What, if anything, might have constituted a set of broadly shared ideas brought from Africa in the realm of kinship? Tentatively and provisionally, we would suggest that there may have been certain widespread fundamental ideas and assumptions about kinship in West and Central Africa. Among these, we might single out the sheer importance of kinship in structuring interpersonal relations and in defining an individual's place in society; the emphasis on unilineal descent, and the importance to each individual of the resulting lines of kinsmen, living and dead, stretching backward and forward through time; or, on a more abstract level, the use of land as a means of defining both time and descent, with ancestors venerated *locally*, and with history and genealogy both being particularized in specific pieces of ground. The aggregate of newly arrived slaves, though they had been torn from their own local kinship networks, would have continued to view kinship as the normal idiom of social relations. Faced with an absence of real kinsmen, they nevertheless modeled their new social ties upon those of kinship, often borrowing kin terms acquired from their masters to label their relationships with their contemporaries and those older than themselves—"bro," "uncle," "auntie," "gran," etc. But in order for such early attempts to invest social relationships with the symbolism of kinship to be transformed into kinship networks grounded in consanguinity, the first and essential requirement was group stability in time and place, or at least sufficient stability to permit the socialization of offspring within that same group. And it is here that the very real differences among plantations and plantation systems would be relevant.

We are assuming, remember, that in the early contact situations between the enslaved and their owners in the New World, the slaves had to develop their life-ways in the face of terrible and usually inescapable constraints. Institution-building would have involved a continuing consciousness of uneven odds, of the masters' overarching power, and of the need to generate social forms that would be adaptive, even under these immensely difficult conditions. In arguing this way, we do not mean to undervalue the importance of the African backgrounds of the slaves or to imply that the slaves knew little, or remembered little, of their heritages. But we do think it reasonable to suppose that the precise ways in which those pasts could be drawn upon to generate new institutions would depend in part upon the particular circumstances in which the slaves found themselves in the New World—the extent to which the slavery regime controlled, interfered with, or interdicted the re-creation of institutional solutions, the stability afforded a particular slave group in its new setting, and so forth. While it would be neat and convenient to suppose that such variables can be ordered according to the aims and values of the master group in specific colonies (e.g., Spanish planters versus English planters, or Jamaica versus Cuba), we do not take up this mode of analysis in the present work.[12]

We might cite one case, however, in which there is evidence that plantation complements achieved considerable stability in early colonial times—the Para region of Suriname. It was the planters' policy here, as elsewhere in Suriname during the first hundred years of the colony's history, not to break up slave families by selling members to different masters, and special care seems to have been taken to avoid separating mothers and children.[13] Over the course of several generations in this region, important kinship groups, each with strong attachments to a particular locality, developed. These were nonunilineal descent groups, composed of *all* the descendants (traced bilaterally) of a particular person who had come from Africa. After several generations, then, any individual would have belonged to a number of such kin groups.

We would contend that these groups, based on cognatic rather than unilineal descent, developed in a social situation in which there were few if any "tasks" for corporate groups to carry out *other than* those relating to ancestor rites.[14] In our view, these groups, which developed during the first several generations of settlement, grew out of the social interaction and common ritual concerns among the descendants of each of the original enslaved Africans. This ritual focus, in turn, was related to widely shared ideas about the importance of kinship in structuring social relations and the central role of ancestors in the ongoing life of the community. Since maximal numbers of descendants would have been desirable for carrying out such rites, and group overlap would pose no problems, there would have been no question of applying restrictive rules for group membership. (We remind the reader that a system based on cognatic descent is able to maximize the number of people who belong to each group, in contrast to a system based on unilineal principles—whether patrilineality or matrilineality—which by definition restricts membership to only *some* of a focal ancestor's descendants.[15]) Over the course of time these Para kin groups, originally focused purely on rites for their collective ancestors (who were buried locally), seem gradually to have taken on a broader function, playing an important role in defining lines of authority and cooperation and in regulating social relations more generally.

An interesting contrast is provided by the Saramaka Maroons, many of whose ancestors escaped from the plantations of the Para region during early colonial times. Their original social groups, composed of slaves who ran away from the same plantation (or who grouped themselves together, at the outset, in the forest) often spent years in relative isolation from one another. These small communities were organized as fighting bands, struggling to forge an independent way of life against tremendous odds.[16] Initially, these groups were mutually suspicious and often hostile, and they were fiercely proud of their own group's skills, knowledge, and accomplishments; moreover, it is probable that they began to hold land corporately almost from the beginning. By the time they had regularized social relations (including marriage) with one another, then, each group had a firm sense of community. We would contend that it was this initial sense of corporateness and the desire to perpetuate it that prompted Saramaka groups, in contrast to the slaves on Para plantations, to adopt a principle of descent (in this case, matrilineality),[17] which restricted an individual's membership to a single group. As in Para, however, the principle of descent was sanctioned by a whole complex of ritual and belief, the collective ancestors became anchored strongly to the soil, and time and space were merged symbolically in the cult of the ancestors.

On the relatively stable plantations of Para, there also developed a strong sense of community, though it came about more gradually than in the case of Saramaka groups. The growth of interlocking kinship ties among the slaves on each plantation certainly contributed to this sense of group solidarity.[18] Each local plantation developed a distinctive character, almost a "micro-culture" of its own, as seen even in their having slightly different styles of drumming to summon their gods; and there were frequent rivalries and feuds among their respective slave complements.[19] Upon Emancipation, the former slaves of the Para region chose to remain where they had always lived and to purchase their plantations communally. We would suggest that it was because the nonexclusive (cognatic) kin-groups of these people (1) would not function efficiently to hold land in common, and (2) by this time were so strongly institutionalized that a switch to a Saramaka-like unilineal system was out of the question, so that a different solution was reached. Here the plantation communities themselves became the land-holding corporations, with individuals gaining rights to land use through their genealogical connections to ancestors who had lived there. Kinship retained, and still retains, its central role in Para social organization, with the principles of descent and ancestry richly particularized and anchored in the land. But in terms of defining the social world of the individual, kinship is accompanied by a concept of community the roots of which are firmly in the New World and, more specifically, in a distinctive form of plantation slavery.

We have seen that the early history of the Saramaka Maroons and that of the original slaves in Para was similar, in that both witnessed considerable stability of personnel through time and a consequent proliferation of genealogical ties. In each case, kinship became a major organizing force in social relations, descent and veneration of the ancestors became a central feature of the religious system, and a strong relationship developed between notions of descent and locality. The ways that these systems came to differ, in our view, can be traced to the fact that initially the people on any Para plantation were merely an "aggregate," while those in Saramaka came to think of themselves, almost from the beginning, as members of particular groups. Although a full comparative analysis of these two kinship systems through time would obviously require a great deal of additional documentation and discussion, we believe that the kinds of variables we have singled out would figure importantly in such an enterprise.

We wish we had examples of other plantation areas where circumstances fostered relative stability of personnel, in order to examine the nature of developing kinship institutions in those settings. One potentially revealing case is Carriacou, in the southeastern Caribbean, where the relative stability of slave personnel was reinforced by the tiny size of the island. Today, we find there the most fully articulated system of unilineal descent (other than that of the Suriname Maroons) in all of Afro-America, replete with a complex ancestor cult and functioning localized patrilineages.[20] At this point, however, our lack of detailed knowledge about the early history of this island, and our even greater ignorance of the development of its people's kinship institutions[21] permit little more than a guess that the variables operating in Suriname may also have been relevant here.

The relative stability and continuity of the slave force on plantations in Suriname (and, perhaps, Carriacou) undoubtedly represents one extreme in the total spectrum of early Afro-America. We are also sure that there were those plantations on which mothers and children were separated almost routinely, where "marriages" were brief at best, and where the slave complement was in a constant state of instability and flux. In such a case (and Saint-Domingue or Jamaica must have had many such estates at certain times in their history), the development of meaningful genealogical ties would have been severely restricted.[22] One imagines that the matricentral cell, composed of a mother and her children,[23] would often have constituted the practical limits of an individual's kinship network. Relations other than those between a mother and her children, and between siblings who grew up together, would likely have been haphazard; lasting ties of paternity or collateral extension (to cousins, uncles, or aunts) might well have been the exception rather than the rule. No matter how strongly the slaves may have *wished* to use the kinship idiom in defining their social relations, in the face of the kind of instability we postulate here they would have had great difficulty developing meaningful groups of kinsmen. With the passage of time, the very notion of kinship as an important organizing force may have lost some of its power, with other kinds of principles (e.g. dyadic, peer-type ties such as "mati") supplementing or partly supplanting those based on kinship. We know that even in nineteenth-century Jamaica, slaves were still using kin terms as honorifics in address: "Among the Negroes it is almost tantamount to an affront to address by name without affixing some term of relationship such as 'grannie' or 'uncle' or 'cousin.' My Cornwall boy, George, told me one day that 'Uncle Sully' wanted to speak to massa. 'Why, is Sully your uncle George?' 'No massa; me only call him so for honour.' "[24]

Our intent is not to underplay the importance of the tiny "family" groups which were often able to form in such systems. In spite of the difficulties these slaves faced in creating stable unions and keeping them together, we have ample evidence of small groups of kinsmen (often simply a woman, her children, and her current spouse) which were basic units of economic cooperation.[25] As we noted earlier, provision-plot agriculture was frequently encouraged by the masters, since it served to reduce plantation costs. Over time, it became sufficiently institutionalized in some slave societies so that the masters might accept as custom the slaves' property rights in their produce and, in an admittedly different sense, their rights in the land they cultivated. An observant eighteenth-century writer on Jamaica, for instance, indicates that the slaves could even "bequeath their grounds or gardens to such of their fellow-slaves as they think proper," though of course the land belonged to the plantation, and never became the slave's property in fee simple.[26]

Though the evidence is scanty, some authors writing on eighteenth-century and early nineteenth-century Jamaica do describe *families* at work on these plots.[27] The marketing of surpluses by slaves, in both Jamaica and Saint-Domingue, appears early in the record,[28] and it is clear that the profits from such enterprise belonged to the slaves themselves, in accord with accepted custom.[29] Hence, in spite of the lengthy and unquestionable record of the oppression of slaves in these societies, we find substantial information on their opportunities to engage in relatively independent economic activity on their own account, and at least some information suggesting that kin groups carried out such activity cooperatively. Beckford, for instance, writing on Jamaica, mentions how the slaves at work on their grounds "move, with all their family, into the place of cultivation; the children of different ages are loaded with baskets, which are burdened in proportion to their strength and age . . . The infants are flung at the backs of the mothers, and very little incommode them in their walks or labour."[30] Patterson even asserts that "the mother gained the labour of her child in working her *provision ground* [italics added; we could find no evidence that provision grounds were granted to women] and later, might even control the extra provision ground given to her children when they had attained adulthood."[31] Even more striking is Patterson's claim that "slave mothers did everything to keep their children within their household and to discourage any attempt at forming permanent unions outside, one nineteenth-century writer stating that to be the main reason for the lack of stable unions among the slaves."[32] Such evidence supports our contention, then, that very small kin groups, which provided a basis for economic cooperation, were able to develop within even some of the most oppressive slave systems.

Given the highly restricted nature of kinship in these slave systems and the limited possibilities for the development of ties other than those between mothers and children and between siblings, Davenport's summary of the major features of (five) modern Caribbean kinship systems takes on special meaning. "We seem to be dealing with systems in which lineal and sibling relations are the only important ones. In contrast to these, avuncular-nepotic and more distant collateral relationships are of secondary importance. By this is meant that the relationship of ego to his grandparents, his parents, and his siblings are the only ones to which rights, duties and obligations are precisely defined, regardless of other considerations."[33] The juxtaposition of Davenport's comments on kinship in contemporary Caribbean societies with our own, relating to the colonial period, is no more than suggestive. Yet we believe that, given sufficient data, it might well be possible to trace direct continuities between the limited growth of kinship institutions in these more heavily industrialized, mobile plantation forces of, say, the eighteenth-century Caribbean, and current forms of social organization in these same areas.

In so doing, however, one might well be surprised by the extent to which people may keep alive, even under conditions of extreme repression, the kinds of fundamental ideas about kinship which we postulated as being widespread in West and Central Africa. After Emancipation in Jamaica, for example, once individuals had gained access to land ownership, large kinship groups which may have been built in at least some ways upon African models, began to take shape in some areas of the island. Composed in theory of all the descendants of the original title holder (traced bilaterally), these late-emerging nonunilineal kinship groups, which were centered on "family land," grew to resemble in certain ways those of the Para region of Suriname, with a ritual association between ancestors and the land on which they were buried.[34] Haiti witnessed a similar development following the slaves' acquisition of land in the early nineteenth century. In some areas, groups of patrikin— coresidential units called *lakou*—grew up around parcels of land, each of which contained an ancestral shrine and was inhabited by particular deities associated with the group.[35] A good deal remains obscure about the precise nature of the kin groups involved in both the Haitian and Jamaican cases. But the existence of such groups suggests that ideas—whether about kinship or other aspects of life—can be kept alive even under severely repressive conditions, and that the nature of particular African-American systems of kinship—or other institutions—cannot be understood except in terms of an extremely variable and complex range of social and economic situations.

To turn our attention to a more specialized aspect of family life, that of the role expectations between spouses, we again confront the need for greater analytical subtlety and more sociohistorical research. We have already noted that a major effect of enslavement was the nearly total destruction of the antecedent statuses held by individuals in the ancestral societies from which they had been torn. In spite of occasional mentions of former status distinctions being observed in the case of particular slaves by those around them—the much romanticized idea of the enslaved prince or princess—it is not at all difficult to perceive why antecedent distinctions of rank would tend to become irrelevant or totally transformed in the plantation setting. However, among such distinctions, those drawn according to sex and age merit special attention in this case, since these biological dimensions against which differences can be calibrated are employed universally in allocating status and role. In Africa as elsewhere, distinctions were drawn between male and female, as well as between young and old, and a good deal of the channeling of life activities originated in these sociological orderings, based on socially learned perceptions of biological differences. We do not feel prepared to assess the variability of African social systems in terms of how they dealt with such differences, but we would like to speculate on plantation slavery's effects on the definition of sex roles.

Earlier we suggested that, to a considerable extent, the slaves on a particular plantation or other colonial enterprise were able to create their own rules and to attempt to live by them—often without significant interference by the masters. But we also stressed the limiting effects of such interference, which was always a possibility and, often enough, a reality. Nowhere was the balance between autonomy and submission more movingly revealed than in the quality of slave domestic life, since it was within the confines of the slave huts and barracks that so much of the most intimate aspects of that life—sexuality, reproduction, birth, socialization, death, love, and hate—was lived out. We recognize that the ultimate power of the masters over the slaves—not only over their lives, but also over their sexuality and its exercise—probably conditioned every aspect of the relationships between men and women. However, while many authors have contended with good reason that slave morality is ultimately referable to the morality of the master class, we suggest once more that the code of the masters set the limits more than it determined the contents of that morality. From the point of view of the masters, of course, individual slaves theoretically had no power over each other, since all were ultimately accountable to their own owners. But we would take the position that this generality is not particularly useful in examining the everyday realities of slave life.

Orlando Patterson has asserted that "slavery abolished any real social distribution between males and females."[36] While we believe he is right to stress that the primary locus of power lay with the planters, we also believe that the evidence about the sexual division of labor belies so sweeping a generalization. As we have indicated, in many of the colonies in which provision-plot agriculture became institutionalized, slaves were permitted to carry their own produce to market. The division of labor with regard to marketing before Emancipation is not well documented. In the case of both Jamaica and Saint-Domingue, however, there are no known descriptions of independent women marketers. Descriptions refer only to unattached males or to family groups. This contrasts sharply with what is known for post-Emancipation Jamaica and postrevolutionary Haiti, for women emerged as the overwhelming majority of marketers in both societies. This development is all the more striking since women are today—and presumably have long been—the marketers in many (perhaps most) West African societies. Indeed, it has sometimes been argued that the predominance of women in contemporary Antillean internal market systems is to be explained by reference to the African past.[37]

Thus a puzzle is posed by the data: that of explaining what might appear to be a "reversion" to the African past, so far as the sexual division of labor is concerned, after lengthy periods during which women appear not to have been independent marketers in these societies. Though we do not feel ready to offer a satisfactory explanation here, we would like to make some comments which may point toward a better understanding of the problem. Upon Emancipation, men seem predominantly to have taken over agricultural production in all of these areas, in spite of the fact that both men and women had worked provision grounds and done field labor during slavery. This male takeover of agriculture may represent an adaptation to the sex-role expectations of the broader European society or it may have some other explanation.[38] The female adaptation to marketing, however, poses a more puzzling problem, since it presumably would have occurred only if the existing role expectations were compatible with the exercise of considerable female autonomy. Simple acquisition of more land by men could not be expected to result in female domination of trade, if such domination ran counter to male notions of masculine dignity or prestige. Husbands had to be willing to permit their wives to engage in economic activities away from the home and, in some cases, even to develop independent careers as marketers.[39]

We remind ourselves here that the idea that a man's masculinity need in no way be diminished by his wife's economic independence was not a standard part of the Western cultural heritage. Many interpretations of family life, both past and present, carry implicit postulates concerning the relationship between men and women (husbands and wives) that preclude a division of authority based on a separation of economic activity. Even in the United States, women who insist on banking their incomes separately have until recent decades been considered inappropriately unfamilistic in most circles.

In this context, it seems clear that the independence and authority exercised by a Haitian or Jamaican market woman in regard to her uses of her own capital probably have few parallels in the Western world, where individual prerogatives commonly are assumed to flow from individual male wealth, embedded in an economically indivisible nuclear family structure. The generation of separate and independent economic risk structures within a single family may be considered characteristically West African and Afro-Caribbean, as opposed to European or North American.[40]

We are not able yet to disaggregate the significance of the African past and the experience of slavery in fostering and nurturing these characteristic Caribbean sex-role expectations. One might wish to argue that, under slavery, with both men and women treated as property, Jamaican and Haitian males were forced to tolerate female autonomy and gradually came to expect it; and that furthermore, upon Emancipation, Jamaican and Haitian females found themselves in a position to exercise more fully that autonomy, in ways remarkably consistent with those of their West African sisters. However, the case of the Saramaka Maroons of Suriname suggests, at least, that this explanation may be insufficient. Though Saramaka women are in many respects strongly dependent economically on men, and have been for centuries, the *idea* that a man's masculinity or status is not tied to his wife's dependence (or lack of it) is as strong here as elsewhere in the Caribbean. Since the original New World ancestors of the Saramaka spent relatively little time as slaves, we can be skeptical that their ideas about sex roles were the product of the plantation experience. If such ideas hold, then, in Saramaka as in Jamaica and Haiti, in spite of their societies' differing divisions of labor, and in spite of the fact that Saramakas had little experience as slaves, the possibility is at least raised that certain fundamental West and Central African concepts about appropriate male and female behavior are involved. In fact, of course, we do not know enough about seventeenth- and eighteenth-century West or Central African societies to make generalizations on this point. Again, we have come up against a fairly subtle level of cultural expectations, akin to "cognitive orientations," on which we, at least, know of little definitive data. However, we might entertain, as a very tentative hypothesis, the idea that certain African notions about the relative separateness of male-female roles were reinforced by the plantation experience, to produce what seem to be characteristic African-American patterns.

We think this example indicates that either-or formulations may no longer have a significant place in Afro-Americanist research. We have at least suggested that surface analogies (e.g., female marketing in West Africa and the Caribbean) will not succeed in revealing as much as less precisely defined but more critical continuities (e.g., male-female attitudes toward individual autonomy). To some extent, the question may be one of the differences among the statuses of male, female, husband and wife, and the status of the individual. To what degree is one's status as an individual compromised by increased emphasis on sex-based status? Again, to what degree is one's status as an individual compromised by the European emphasis on the statuses of husband and wife? It is obvious that we have no answers; but we believe that the questions are intimately connected to the emergence of the particular status systems that typify African-American societies.

7
CONCLUSION

〜〜〜

We have sought here to propose an approach to the study of African-American societies and cultures which refines—rather than discards or disproves—earlier approaches. Our central thesis is simple: that continuities between the Old World and the New must be established upon an understanding of the basic conditions under which the migrations of enslaved Africans occurred. To support this thesis, we have employed both documentary materials and speculation to describe those conditions and to suggest some of the social processes at work in the early confrontations between Europeans and Africans.

We are not prepared to analyze these processes, either by assuming that the African societies which contributed peoples and cultural heritages to the building of Afro-America were homogeneous, or by assuming that any New World colony was peopled primarily by migrants from some single African society. Nor are we content to ignore the difference between social-relational and cultural perspectives in understanding what really happened, since we understand the proliferation of new social institutions under slavery to be the precondition and basis for continuities in culture. Our view of the free and slave sectors as deeply divided from each other, yet profoundly interdependent, is critical to our understanding of how such institution-building took place. As we have contended, some of these institutions were rooted in the relationships between the two sectors; others, even more important to our argument here, developed largely within the slave sector, though always subject to outer limits of variability imposed by the society at large. Thus, when seen from the vantage-point of daily social interaction, slave institutions do appear to assume in some fashion a concentric order, extending from the immediate interpersonal links between two persons, through the domestic and familial ties of larger groupings, and outward to the religious, economic, and other institutions that bound slave communities together. The institutions linking enslaved and free people constitute a different order, or dimension, of social action, since the linkages inevitably crossed the chasm between the sectors. But as we have sought to stress, these are not different orders or dimensions in the sense that they were totally separate; such separation was more apparent than real, so far as day-to-day life was concerned.

African-American social and cultural forms were forged in the fires of enslavement, but these forms could not, and cannot, be defined by confining them to those peoples or societies whose physical origins were African any more than Euro-American social and cultural forms are limited to those whose physical origins were European. The eminent historian of the American South, C. Vann Woodward, is close to the truth when he asserts that "so far as their culture is concerned, all Americans are part Negro."[1] Some would prefer to say "part African" and others "part black"; in any case, we stand with

Herskovits: "whether Negroes borrowed from whites or whites from Negroes, in this or any other aspect of culture, it must always be remembered that the borrowing was never achieved without resultant change in whatever was borrowed, and, in addition, without incorporating elements which originated in the new habits that, as much as anything else, give the new form its distinctive quality."[2] As we have sought to suggest, "borrowing" may not best express the reality at all—"creating" or "remodeling" may be more precise.

We regard few of our contentions as proved or even certain. The test of their validity, in fact, should rest more with the tasks of serious historical and anthropological research, and far less with their persuasiveness on logical, ideological, or sentimental grounds. Indeed we suspect that our arguments can be pressed into service for quite different *partis-pris*, much as occurred with the positions taken by our predecessors in the study of Afro-America. The inescapable fact in the study of Afro-America is the humanity of the oppressed, and the inhumanity of the systems that oppressed them. But not all slavery systems oppressed all slaves equally, and not all slaves dealt with their oppression in the same ways. We have attempted here to suggest certain research directions that might prove fruitful in the examination of contemporary African-American societies by ethnographic procedures, and the histories of such societies, through the use of documents, historical records, and the recollections of living people. It is our concern to support our contention that the people in African-American societies, in which oppression was pervasive, quite literally built their life-ways to meet their daily needs.

The general theoretical position we take in this essay is that the past must be viewed as the conditioning circumstance of the present. We do not believe that the present can be "understood"—in the sense of explaining the relationships among different contemporary institutional forms—without reference to the past. We suppose this to be the case, whether our interest be in the European peoples who conquered the world they called "new," the Indian peoples they destroyed and subjugated with it, or the African—and, later, Asian—peoples they dragged into it. New World it is, for those who became its peoples remade it, and in the process, they remade themselves.

NOTES

~~~~~~~~

PREFACE

1. For an excellent bibliographical review of this period, see Peter H. Wood, " 'I did the best I could for my day': The study of early Black history during the Second Reconstruction, 1960 to 1976," *William & Mary Quarterly* 35 (1978): 185–225. For a review of subsequent work on slavery, see Joseph C. Miller, *Slavery: A Worldwide Bibliography, 1900–1982* (White Plains, NY: Kraus International, 1985), and the ongoing supplements by Miller, Larissa V. Brown, James V. Skalnik, and David F. Appleby, published in the journal *Slavery and Abolition.*

2. Mervyn C. Alleyne, *Roots of Jamaican Culture* (London: Pluto Press, 1988): 4–5, 17–23, *et passim.*

3. Daniel J. Crowley, review of S. and R. Price, *Afro-American Arts of the Suriname Rain Forest,* in *African Arts* 16 (1981): 27, 80–81.

4. J. L. Dillard, *Black Names* (The Hague: Mouton, 1976): 10–11.

5. Joseph E. Holloway, "The origins of African-American culture," in *Africanisms in American Culture,* ed. Joseph E. Holloway (Bloomington: Indiana University Press, 1990): xi. Since the book's original subtitle was *A Caribbean Perspective,* criticisms of our geographical focus strike us as misdirected.

6. Charles Joyner, "Creolization," in *Encyclopedia of Southern Culture,*

ed. Charles Reagan Wilson and William Ferris (Chapel Hill: University of North Carolina Press, 1989): 147–49; C. Vann Woodward, "The narcissistic South," *New York Review of Books* (October 26, 1989): 13–14, 16–17; Charles Joyner, "Speaking Southern," *New York Review of Books* (February 15, 1989): 52–53; C. Vann Woodward, *ibid.*

7. The photo and caption appear in Walter Jackson, "Melville Herskovits and the search for Afro-American culture," in *Malinowski, Rivers, Benedict and Others: Essays on Culture and Personality*, ed. George W. Stocking, Jr. (Madison: University of Wisconsin Press, 1986): 96.

8. Lawrence W. Levine, *Black Culture and Black Consciousness: Afro-American Folk Thought from Slavery to Freedom* (New York: Oxford University Press, 1977); Henry Louis Gates, Jr., *The Signifying Monkey: A Theory of Afro-American Literary Criticism* (New York: Oxford University Press, 1988); Sandra T. Barnes, ed., *Africa's Ogun: Old World and New* (Bloomington: Indiana University Press, 1989).

9. "Several art histories, not one, flourish today upon our planet. The creole thing to do is to mix them. Gone is the notion of a single canon. Bring on the Callaloo." Robert Farris Thompson, "Recapturing heaven's glamour: Afro-Caribbean festivalizing arts," in *Caribbean Festival Arts*, ed. John W. Nunley and Judith Bettelheim (Seattle: University of Washington Press, 1988): 17–29.

10. David H. Brown, *Garden in the Machine: Afro-Cuban Sacred Art and Performance in Urban New Jersey and New York.* Ph.D. dissertation, Yale University, 1989.

11. Edward Kamau Brathwaite, *Folk Culture of the Slaves in Jamaica*, rev. ed. (London: New Beacon Books, 1981): 6–7.

12. Melville J. Herskovits, *Life in a Haitian Valley* (New York: Knopf, 1937): 303–304.

INTRODUCTION

1. A. P. Newton, *The European Nations in the West Indies, 1493–1688* (London: A. & C. Black, 1933); V. T. Harlow, *A History of Barbados, 1625–1685* (Oxford: Oxford University Press, 1926); Gabriel Debien, "Les engagés pour les Antilles (1634–1715)," *Revue d'Histoire des Colonies* 38 (1951): 7–277; Jerome S. Handler, "The Amerindian slave population of Barbados in the seventeenth and early eighteenth centuries," *Caribbean Studies* 8(4) (1969): 38–64.

1. THE ENCOUNTER MODEL

1. H. Hoetink, *The Two Variants in Caribbean Race Relations* (London: Oxford University Press, 1967): 111 *et seq.*

2. The relative cultural homogeneity or heterogeneity of African peoples in their ancestral homeland, as compared with that of the Europeans, is not at issue here. What we would stress is that enslaved Africans were usually randomized (or in some cases even deliberately heterogenized) by enslavement, transportation, and seasoning so as to make their initial New World experience very different from that of the Europeans.

3. Melville J. Herskovits, *The Myth of the Negro Past* (1941; reprint, Boston: Beacon Press, 1990): 81–85.

4. See, for example, P. C. Lloyd, *Africa in Social Change* (Baltimore: Penguin, 1972): 25–27, and T. O. Ranger, "Recent developments in the study of African religious and cultural history and their relevance for the historiography of the Diaspora," *Ufahamu* 4(2) (1973): 17–34. M. G. Smith offers one of the more extreme statements of this position: "[T]he types of ambiguity which lurk within the unitary concept of an African inheritance are great indeed . . . [It] presupposes a uniformity and uniqueness of African cultures which ethnography does not support . . . [There are] marked cultural dissimilarities within the West African regions from which the bulk of Caribbean Negroes trace descent. Even when the influence of Islam in this area is excluded, there remain sufficiently important differences of culture for reference to or definition of a cultural pattern as characteristic of this area to remain highly suspect." M. G. Smith, "The African heritage in the Caribbean," in *Caribbean Studies: A Symposium*, ed. V. Rubin (Seattle: University of Washington Press, 1957): 36, 39–40.

5. George M. Foster, "Peasant society and the image of limited good," *American Anthropologist* 67 (1965): 293.

6. Robert F. Thompson, *Black Gods and Kings*, Occasional Papers of the Museum and Laboratories of Ethnic Arts and Technology (Los Angeles: University of California, 1971): ch. 13, 1–5.

7. Victor C. Uchendu, *The Igbo of Southeast Nigeria* (New York: Holt, Rinehart and Winston, 1965): 58.

8. See, for example, Alan Lomax, "The homogeneity of African-Afro-American musical style," in *Afro-American Anthropology*, ed. N. Whitten

and J. Szwed (New York: Free Press, 1970): 181–201; Alan P. Merriam, "African music," in *Continuity and Change in African Cultures*, ed. William R. Bascom and Melville J. Herskovits (Chicago: University of Chicago Press, 1959): 49–86; J. H. Kwabena Nketia, "African music," in *Peoples and Cultures of Africa*, ed. E. P. Skinner (Garden City: Natural History Press, 1973): 580–99; Robert P. Armstrong, *The Affecting Presence* (Urbana: University of Illinois Press, 1971); Robert F. Thompson, "An aesthetic of the cool: West African dance," *African Forum* 2(2) (1966): 85–102; and Roger D. Abrahams, "The shaping of folklore traditions in the British West Indies," *Journal of Inter-American Studies* 9 (1967): 456–80.

9. Herskovits, *Myth of the Negro Past*: 81.

10. Melville J. Herskovits, "Some psychological implications of Afroamerican studies," in *Acculturation in the Americas*, ed. Sol Tax (Chicago: University of Chicago Press, 1952): 153 (his italics); 153–55.

11. George E. Simpson, "Afro-American religions and religious behavior," *Caribbean Studies* 12(2) (1972): 12.

12. David Dalby, "The African element in American English," in *Rappin' and Stylin' Out: Communication in Urban Black America*, ed. T. Kochman (Urbana: University of Illinois Press, 1972): 173.

13. See, for instance, Alfred L. Kroeber, *Cultural and Natural Areas of Native North America*, University of California Publications in American Archeology and Ethnology 38 (Berkeley: University of California Press, 1939).

14. Melville J. Herskovits, "A preliminary consideration of the culture areas of Africa," *American Anthropologist* 26 (1924): 50–63.

15. See, for instance, Melville J. Herskovits, *Man and His Works* (New York: Knopf, 1948).

16. Melville J. Herskovits, *Acculturation: The Study of Culture Contact* (New York: J. J. Augustin, 1938); Herskovits, "Introduction," in Tax, ed., *Acculturation in the Americas*, 48–63; Robert Redfield, Ralph Linton, and Melville J. Herskovits, "Memorandum for the study of acculturation," *American Anthropologist* 38 (1936): 149–52.

17. See, for example, Melville J. Herskovits, "Problem, method and theory in Afroamerican studies," *Afroamérica* 1 (1945): 5–24.

18. See Dieudonné Rinchon, *Le trafic négrier* (Brussels: Atlas, 1938);

Gabriel Debien, "Les origines des esclaves des Antilles," *Bulletin de l'Institut Français d'Afrique Noire* 23, sér. B., nos. 3–4 (1961): 363–87; *idem*, "Les origines des esclaves des Antilles," *Bulletin de l'Institut Français d'Afrique Noire* 27, sér. B, nos. 3–4 (1965): 755–99; *idem*, "Les origines des esclaves aux Antilles," *Bulletin de l'Institut Français d'Afrique Noire* 24, sér. B, nos. 3–4 (1967): 536–58; M. Delafosse and G. Debien, "Les origines des esclaves aux Antilles," *Bulletin de l'Institut Français d'Afrique Noire*, 27, sér. B, nos. 1–2 (1965): 319–69; J. Houdaille, "Les origines des esclaves des Antilles," *Bulletin de l'Institut Français d'Afrique Noire* 26, sér. B, nos. 3–4 (1964): 601–675; and J. Houdaille, R. Massio, and G. Debien, "Les origines des esclaves des Antilles," *Bulletin de l'Institut Français d'Afrique Noire* 25, sér. B, nos. 3–4 (1963): 215–65.

19. Philip Curtin, *The Atlantic Slave Trade: A Census* (Madison: University of Wisconsin Press, 1969).

20. Francois Girod, *De la société créole: Saint-Domingue au 18ᵉ siècle* (Paris: Hachette, 1972): 123.

21. Jean Fouchard, *Les marrons de la liberté* (Paris: Editions de l'Ecole, 1972): 183–89.

22. For details, see Richard Price, "KiKoongo and Saramaccan: A reappraisal," *Bijdragen tot de Taal-, Land-, en Volkenkunde* 131 (1975): 461–78; *idem, The Guiana Maroons: A Historical and Bibliographical Introduction* (Baltimore and London: The Johns Hopkins University Press, 1976). We do not mean to contend that absolute numbers were the only, or necessarily the most important, determinant of the particular forms cultural development would take in these situations. In fact, our contention is more to the contrary: quite apart from much more careful research on the precise composition of migrant groups in particular locales at particular points in time, we need to examine very carefully whatever is available concerning the specific social contexts within which cultural innovation and perpetuation could occur. We recognize—as we shall later make clear—that even single individuals might make a disproportionately large contribution to the evolution of specific forms.

23. Angelina Pollak-Eltz, *Afro-Amerikaanse godsdiensten en culten* (Roermond: J. J. Romen en Zonen, 1970): 142.

24. Gwendolyn M. Hall, *Social Control in Slave Plantation Societies* (Baltimore: Johns Hopkins University Press, 1971): 66.

25. Laënnec Hurbon, *Dieu dans le vaudou haïtien* (Paris: Payot, 1972): 73.

26. See, for instance, Roger Bastide, *Les Amériques noires* (Paris: Payot, 1967): 17–19; Pollak-Eltz, *Afro-Amerikaanse godsdiensten*: 68.

27. Herskovits, *Myth of the Negro Past*: 86–87; M. G. Smith, "African heritage": 35.

28. See Mervyn C. Alleyne, "Acculturation and the cultural matrix of creolization," in *Pidginization and Creolization of Languages*, ed. Dell Hymes (Cambridge: Cambridge University Press, 1971): 169–86; David DeCamp, "Introduction: The study of pidgin and creole languages," in Hymes, *Pidginization*: 13–39; Sidney W. Mintz, "The socio-historical background of pidginization and creolization," in Hymes, *Pidginization*: 153–68.

29. Dell Hymes, *Foundations in Sociolinguistics: An Ethnographic Approach* (Philadelphia: University of Pennsylvania Press, 1974); William Labov, *Sociolinguistic Patterns* (Philadelphia: University of Pennsylvania Press, 1972).

2. SOCIOCULTURAL CONTACT AND FLOW IN SLAVE SOCIETIES

1. Roy S. Bryce-Laporte, "The slave plantation: background to present conditions of urban blacks," in *Race, Change and Urban Society*, Urban Affairs Annual Reviews 5, ed. P. Orleans and W. R. Ellis (Beverly Hills: Sage, 1971): 265–66.

2. Douglas Hall writes:

The economic reference was an inseparable aspect of a total human relationship. Thus the essential and unanswerable problem of estate slavery was that although the slaves were accounted as capital equipment they were people, and their masters were torn by conflict between these two views of their property. Unlike the sugarmill, and even [sic!] unlike the horse to which an owner might feel some sentimental attachment, and which might obviously return affection, the slave had also a social status, and a capacity to organize and to provide for himself if the opportunity were allowed.

Douglas Hall, "Slaves and slavery in the British West Indies," *Social and Economic Studies* 11(4) (1962): 309.

3. See Edward Long, *The History of Jamaica* (London: T. Lowndes, 1774); Sidney W. Mintz, "Currency problems in eighteenth-century Jamaica and Gresham's Law," in *Patterns and Processes in Culture,* ed. R. Manners (Chicago: Aldine, 1964): 248–65; *idem, Caribbean Transformations* (1974; 2nd ed., New York: Columbia University Press, 1989).

4. See Roy S. Bryce-Laporte, "Slaves as inmates, slaves as men: a sociological discussion of Elkins' thesis," in *The Debate on Slavery,* ed. A. Lane (Urbana: University of Illinois Press, 1971): 269–92.

5. R. A. J. van Lier, *Frontier Society: A Social Analysis of the History of Surinam,* Koninklijk Instituut voor Taal-, Land- en Volkenkunde, trans. ser. 14 (The Hague: Martinus Nijhoff, 1971): 76–77.

6. A comparable case is reported from early nineteenth-century Barbados: "I was once rallying a Barbadian [white creole] upon his circumstance (certainly of very rare occurrence), which at that time was much talked of in the island; namely, an intrigue detected between a young lady and one of her father's slaves, an African negro lately imported." J. A. Waller, *A Voyage to the West Indies* (London: Sir Richard Phillips and Company, 1820): 96–97. Similar Jamaican examples are cited in Orlando Patterson, "Slavery and slave revolts: A sociohistorical analysis of the First Maroon War, 1655–1740," *Social and Economic Studies* 19 (1970): 322; and Edward Kamau Brathwaite, *The Development of Creole Society in Jamaica, 1770–1820* (Oxford: Clarendon Press, 1971): 188–91.

7. Sidney W. Mintz, "Groups, group boundaries, and the perception of race," *Comparative Studies in Society and History* 13 (1971): 437–43.

8. It even seems that the religion and medicine of the slaves played an important role, in some colonies, in the lives of the whites. Writing of Suriname, Van Lier notes: "It is apparent from the *Essai Historique* [1788] that in cases of illness Europeans often consulted the witch doctors [sic] of the Negroes. A number of cases of Europeans exercising pressure on converted [Christian] slaves who formerly enjoyed some fame as experts in this field to revert to their former practices are also mentioned." Van Lier, *Frontier Society:* 83–84. Henock Trouillot refers to the paramedical roles of slaves in Saint-Domingue and cites Descourtilz's preference for black healers to "certain callow quacks which the sea occasionally spews upon the beaches of our colonies." Henock Trouillot, "La condition des travailleurs à Saint-Domingue," *Revue de la Société Haïtienne d'Histoire, de Géographie et de Géologie* 34 (1969): 79–81.

9. Lady Maria Nugent, *Lady Nugent's Journal*, ed. Frank Cundall (1839; London: Institute of Jamaica, 1939): 92, 95, 121, 127, *et passim*.

10. *Ibid.*, 93, 131, 132.

11. Brathwaite, *Development of Creole Society*: 300–305.

12. Nugent, *Journal*: 204.

13. We have made no attempt in this discussion to touch upon the important controversy surrounding the work of Frank Tannenbaum, Stanley Elkins, and others, even though we believe the materials we have covered are relevant. See Frank Tannenbaum, *Slave and Citizen* (New York: Knopf, 1947); Stanley Elkins, *Slavery: A Problem in American Institutional and Intellectual Life* (Chicago: University of Chicago Press, 1959); Ann Lane, ed., *The Debate on Slavery: Stanley Elkins and His Critics* (Urbana: University of Illinois Press, 1971). In our view, the whole complex of relationships between masters and slaves will not yield to simple formulas which require that "the slaves" be viewed either as unremittingly resistant on the one hand, or psychically destroyed on the other. In spite of the great usefulness of large-scale contrasts—and we recognize that much of the work embodied here is precisely of this kind—the need is for careful and specific historical research on particular cases, in particular periods. See Sidney W. Mintz, review of S. Elkins, *Slavery*, in *American Anthropologist* 63 (1961): 579–87; *idem*, "Slavery and the slaves," *Caribbean Studies* 8(4) (1969): 65–70; *idem*, "Toward an Afro-American history," *Cahiers d'Histoire Mondiale* 13 (1971): 317–32; *idem*, *Caribbean Transformations*; Richard Price, ed., *Maroon Societies: Rebel Slave Communities in the Americas* (1973; 2nd ed., Baltimore: Johns Hopkins University Press, 1979); *idem*, *The Guiana Maroons*.

3. THE SLAVE SECTOR

1. James M. Phillippo, *Jamaica: Its Past and Present State* (London: John Snow, 1843): 252.

2. *Ibid.*, 251.

3. This is, admittedly, a simplistic way of summarizing a very complex reality. For instance, we do not attempt to analyze the internal differentiation of the slave group along status lines imposed to some extent by the plantation regimen: the distinctions among "praedial" (field) slaves, domestic slaves, drivers and foremen, artisans, etc., which played an important part in the

organization of slave life. Clearly, many slaves were—by virtue of differential status, occupation, or otherwise—more or less remote from contact with the masters and with transferred European culture. But to attempt to treat such differences adequately in an essay of this length would complicate the presentation excessively.

4. There is probably no more telling illustration of the masters' acceptance of their dependence upon the slaves, even in regards quite separate from plantation labor, than the development of provision grounds and marketing by the slaves, and the customary rights of the slaves that came to be recognized by the planters. Two of the harshest slavery systems in history, in Jamaica and Saint-Domingue, had flourishing systems of subsistence agriculture and of marketplaces, run by slaves in good part. Sidney W. Mintz, "The Jamaican internal marketing pattern," *Social and Economic Studies* 4 (1955): 95–103; Sidney W. Mintz and Douglas Hall, "The origins of the Jamaican internal marketing system," in *Papers in Caribbean Anthropology*, ed. Sidney W. Mintz (New Haven: Yale University Publications in Anthropology 57, 1960); Mintz, "Les roles economiques"; *idem*, "Caribbean marketplaces."

4. THE BEGINNINGS OF AFRICAN-AMERICAN SOCIETIES AND CULTURES

1. J. Stewart, *A View of the Past and Present State of the Island of Jamaica* (Edinburgh: Oliver and Boyd, 1823): 250.

2. J. Kelly, *Voyage to Jamaica and Narrative of 17 years Residence in that Island* (1838), cited in Orlando Patterson, *The Sociology of Slavery* (London: MacGibbon and Kee, 1967): 150.

3. *Ibid.*; see also Orlando Patterson, *Die the Long Day* (New York: John Morrow, 1972): 163–64.

4. Jan Voorhoeve and Ursy M. Lichtveld, *Creole Drum: An Anthology of Creole Literature from Surinam* (New Haven: Yale University Press, 1975): 55.

5. Roger Bastide, *Les religions africaines au Brésil* (Paris: Presses Universitaires de France, 1961): 118–19.

6. Donald Wood, *Trinidad in Transition* (London: Oxford University Press, 1968): 238.

7. Richard Price, *Saramaka Social Structure: Analysis of a Maroon So-

ciety in Surinam, Caribbean Monograph Series, no. 12 (Río Piedras: Institute of Caribbean Studies, 1975): 165; Melville J. Herskovits and Frances S. Herskovits, *Suriname Folk-lore*, Columbia University Contributions to Anthropology, 27 (New York: Columbia University Press, 1936): 32–35.

8. M. L. E. Moreau de Saint-Méry, *Déscription . . . de la partie française de l'isle Saint-Domingue* (1797; Paris: Larose, 1958): 58.

9. Victor Turner has gone farther in these connections, generalizing about symbols in African ritual.

> . . . from the comparative viewpoint, there are remarkable similarities among symbols used in ritual throughout sub-Saharan Africa, in spite of differences in cosmological sophistication. The same ideas, analogies, and modes of association underlie symbol formation and manipulation from the Senegal River to the Cape of Good Hope. The same assumptions about powers prevail in kingdoms and nomadic bands. Whether these assemblages of similar symbols represent units of complex orders or the debris of formerly prevalent ones, the symbols remain extraordinarily viable and the themes they represent and embody tenaciously rooted.

We would emphasize that our attempt to tease out common principles and orientations in West and Central African religious systems is not meant to ignore the obvious fact that these religions differed, and differ, in many ways from one another; in fact, such differences are viewed by us as an essential part of the model we are constructing. Victor W. Turner, "Symbols in African ritual," *Science* 179 (1973): 1105.

10. It should by no means be thought that we mean by this that the rupture with the African past was irrevocable or permanent. We take pains, elsewhere in this essay, to point to immensely important continuities of many kinds with ancestral civilizations; and we must add that the history of Afro-America is marked by renewals of identification on many occasions, and in various forms: sentimental, political, literary, etc. Our stress here is rather upon the disjuncture created by the processes of enslavement and of "heterogenization" that typified transportation and the initial New World situation. As Ralph Ellison has eloquently suggested:

> For as I see it, from the days of their introduction into the colonies, Negroes have taken, with the ruthlessness of those without articulate investments in cultural styles, whatever they could of European music, making of it that which would, when blended with the cultural ten-

dencies inherited from Africa, express their own sense of life—while rejecting the rest. Perhaps this is only another way of saying that whatever the degree of injustice and inequality sustained by the slaves, American culture was, even before the official founding of the nation, pluralistic; and it was the African's origin in cultures in which art was highly functional which gave him an edge in shaping the music and dance of this nation.

Ralph Ellison, *Shadow and Act* (New York: New American Library, 1966): 248.

11. Daniel P. Mannix and Malcolm Cowley, *Black Cargoes: A History of the Atlantic Slave Trade* (New York: Viking, 1965): 114.

12. Capt. John Gabriel Stedman, *Narrative of a Five Years Expedition against the Revolted Negroes of Surinam*, ed. Richard Price and Sally Price (1790; Baltimore and London: Johns Hopkins University Press, 1988): 174.

13. Jan Voorhoeve, "Church creole and pagan cult languages," in Hymes, ed., *Pidginization*: 307; see also Jan Voorhoeve and Ursy M. Lichtveld, *Creole Drum: An Anthology of Creole Literature from Surinam* (New Haven: Yale University Press, 1975).

14. Price, *The Guiana Maroons*; Charles Wooding, *Winti: een Afroamerikaanse godsdienst in Suriname* (Meppel: Krips Repro., 1972).

15. Jerome S. Handler and Charlotte J. Frisbie, "Aspects of slave life in Barbados: music and its cultural context," *Caribbean Studies* 11(4) (1972): 5–40.

16. Some beliefs and rites have always served as a focus of conservatism, a badge of fidelity to the African past. But even for adherents of what Bastide calls (African) *"religions en conserve"* (*Les Amériques noires: 133–55*), such as Cuban *santería* and Bahian *candomblé*, life went on amidst the dynamic, overwhelmingly African-*American* present. If we seem to underemphasize the African past to stress the motile nature of Afro-America, it is in part because the usual emphasis seems to have been the reverse. Moreover, we recognize that many aspects of African-American adaptiveness may themselves be in some important sense African in origin. See Herskovits, *Myth of the Negro Past*: 141–42. Our aim is to lay bare the processes of change somewhat more precisely, not to opt for one or another "explanation" of the roots of Afro-America.

5. RETENTIONS AND SURVIVALS

1. See, for example, Richard Price and Sally Price, "*Kammbá*: the ethnohistory of an Afro-American art," *Antropologica* 32 (1972): 3–27; *idem*, "Saramaka onomastics: an Afro-American naming system," *Ethnology* 11 (1972): 341–67; Sally Price and Richard Price, *Afro-American Arts of the Suriname Rain Forest* (Berkeley and Los Angeles: University of California Press, 1980).

2. Philip J. C. Dark, *Bush Negro Art: An African Art in the Americas* (London: Tiranti, 1954); J. L. Volders, *Bouwkunst in Suriname: Driehonderd jaren nationale architectuur* (Hilversum: G. van Saane, 1966).

3. Robert F. Thompson, "From Africa," *Yale Alumni Magazine* 34 (1970): 18.

4. Jean Hurault, *Africains de Guyane: La vie matérielle et l'art des noirs réfugiés de Guyane* (The Hague: Mouton, 1970); Richard Price, "Saramaka woodcarving: the development of an Afro-american art," *Man* 5 (1970): 363–78; *idem*, "The Guiana maroons: changing perspectives in 'Bush Negro' studies," *Caribbean Studies* 11(4) (1972): 82–105; Price and Price, *Afro-American Arts*.

5. See, for instance, John F. Szwed, "Afro-American musical adaptations," in *Afro-American Anthropology*, ed. N. Whitten and J. Szwed (New York: Free Press, 1970): 219–28; Sally Price, *Co-wives and Calabashes* (Ann Arbor: University of Michigan Press, 1984).

6. Richard Price, "Saramaka emigration and marriage: a case study of social change," *Southwestern Journal of Anthropology* 26 (1970): 157–89; *idem, Saramaka Social Structure*.

7. Gerhard Lindblom, *Afrikanische Relikte und Indianische Entlehnungen in der Kultur der Busch-Neger Surinams* (Göteborg: Elanders Boktryckeri Aktiebolag, 1924): 92–93; John Barbot, "A description of the coasts of North and South-Guinea," in *A Collection of Voyages and Travels* 5, ed. Awnsham Churchill (London, 1732): 373.

8. C. L. Schumann, "Saramaccanisch Deutsches Wörter-Buch," in *Die Sprache der Saramakkaneger in Surinam*, ed. Hugo Schuchardt, Verhandelingen der Koninklijke Akademie van Wetenschappen te Amsterdam 14 (1914): 46–116. s.v. *kangra*.

9. Charles Leslie, *A New History of Jamaica* (London: J. Hodges, 1740):

308–309; Thomas Atwood, *The History of the Island of Dominica* (London: J. Johnson, 1791): 268–69; F. Staehelin, *Die Mission der Brüdergemeine in Suriname und Berbice im achtzehnten Jahrhundert* (Herrnhut: Vereins für Brüdergeschichte in Kommission der Unitätsbuchhandlung in Gnadau, 1913–19, 3(2): 55.

10. Wood, *Trinidad*, 80.

11. K. O. Laurence, *Immigration into the West Indies in the 19th Century* (London: Caribbean Universities Press, 1971): 14.

12. Wood, *Trinidad*, 240–41.

13. Andrew Carr, "A Rada community in Trinidad," *Caribbean Quarterly* 3(1) (n.d. [1953]): 40.

14. Curtin, *Atlantic Slave Trade:* 40, 43.

15. William R. Bascom, "Two forms of Afro-Cuban divination," in *Acculturation in the Americas*, ed. Sol Tax (Chicago: University of Chicago Press, 1952): 172–73; see also Montero de Bascom, "Influencias africanas en la cultura cubana," *Ciencias Sociales* 5 (1954): 98–102.

16. A large but uneven literature deals with African survivals and retentions in the New World. Pioneering works include Herskovits, *Myth of the Negro Past*, and selected essays dating back to 1930 by the same author; see Melville J. Herskovits, *The New World Negro* (Bloomington: Indiana University Press, 1966) and Arthur Ramos, *Las Culturas Negras en el Nuevo Mundo* (Mexico: Fondo de Cultura Económica, 1943). Bastide's *Les Amériques noires* is available in English translation as *African Civilisations in the New World* (New York: Harper and Row, 1971). A useful debate about survivals and retentions is to be found in *Caribbean Studies: A Symposium*, ed. V. Rubin (Seattle: University of Washington Press, 1957), where M. G. Smith exchanges views with George E. Simpson and Peter B. Hammond (pp. 34–53).

6. KINSHIP AND SEX ROLES

1. See, for instance, E. Franklin Frazier, "The Negro in Bahia, Brazil: a problem in method," *American Sociological Review* 7 (1942): 465–78; and Melville J. Herskovits, "The Negro in Bahia, Brazil: a problem in method," *American Sociological Review* 8 (1943): 394–402.

2. Herskovits, *Life in a Haitian Valley* (1937; New York: Doubleday

Anchor, 1971): 260; Melville J. Herskovits and Frances S. Herskovits, *Trinidad Village* (New York: Knopf, 1947): 293.

3. E. Franklin Frazier, *The Negro Family in the United States* (Chicago: University of Chicago Press, 1939): 20; *ibid.*, ch. 1.

4. T. S. Simey, *Welfare and Planning in the West Indies* (Oxford: Clarendon Press, 1946): 49.

5. We cannot examine here the ideological aspects of this controversy, past or present. But it bears noting that, while the "pro-Africanistic" perspective at one time ran the risk of implying that African-Americans were inherently different and therefore unassimilable, the same argument may have quite different connotations today. Both Frazier and Herskovits were well aware of these implications, and one supposes that they would be wryly amused by the course of the debate in its newer form.

6. Keith F. Otterbein, "Caribbean family organization: a comparative analysis," *American Anthropologist* 67 (1965): 66; Michael G. Smith, *West Indian Family Structure* (Seattle: University of Washington Press, 1962): 218.

7. Sidney W. Mintz, "Foreword," in Whitten and Szwed, *Afro-American Anthropology*, 1–16; *idem*, "Creating culture in the Americas," *Columbia University Forum* 13 (1970): 4–11.

8. Richard Price, "Studies of Caribbean family organization: problems and prospects," *Dédalo* 14 (1971): 23–59.

9. Sidney W. Mintz, "Cañamelar: the subculture of a rural sugar plantation proletariat," in *The People of Puerto Rico*, ed. J. H. Steward, *et al.* (Urbana: University of Illinois Press, 1956): 375–77.

10. Chandra Jayawardena, "Family organization in plantations in British Guiana," *International Journal of Comparative Sociology* 3 (1962): 63–64.

11. Meyer Fortes, "Introduction," in *The Developmental Cycle in Domestic Groups*, ed. Jack Goody, Cambridge Papers in Social Anthropology no. 1 (Cambridge: Cambridge University Press, 1958): 1–14; Nancie L. Solien, "Household and family in the Caribbean," *Social and Economic Studies* 9 (1960): 101–106; Sidney Greenfield, "Socio-economic factors and family form," *Social and Economic Studies* 10 (1961): 72–85; Raymond T. Smith, "The nuclear family in Afro-American kinship," *Journal of Comparative Family Studies* 1 (1970): 55–70.

12. We believe that, just as the values, attitudes, and beliefs of the slaves—in short, their "cognitive orientations"—played a critical role in how they dealt with the impact of slavery and the plantation system, so, too, the cognitive orientations of different master classes were a critical factor in the forms of resistance and of institution-building that took place. Many useful and interesting formulations can be attempted on these grounds, contrasting the elaboration of slave institutions in different colonies and at different periods. But we suspect that most such formulations to date have been based on the lack of more detailed historical information, rather than on the persuasiveness of the data. Generalizations about slave society in Jamaica, say, or in Saint-Domingue, necessarily ignore the very considerable sociological variability that must have typified any of these colonies, and the institutional variation among the slaves that probably accompanied this complexity. Whether we have in mind folklore, marriage rules, techniques of resistance, or anything else, our generalizations about "what the slaves did" or "how the slaves thought" obviously are subject to stern qualification. Only a great deal more very careful historical research will ever enable us to handle these problems with the sensitivity they demand.

13. Needless to say, this policy was not based merely on humanitarian grounds but, as we learn from explicit contemporary statements, on the planters' perceptions of their own economic interests. By the late eighteenth century, when economic conditions were different and plantations began to change hands rapidly, families were frequently separated, with planters continuing to justify their actions on the basis of their own economic interests. Van Lier, *Frontier Society:* 154–55.

14. See Ward H. Goodenough, *Description and Comparison in Cultural Anthropology* (Chicago: Aldine, 1970): 52.

15. *Ibid*, 53. We recognize, of course, that nonunilineal groups may restrict membership, making use of criteria other than sex. However, our point here is that in a situation marked by a perceived scarcity of descendants for any particular ancestor, such restrictions would be unlikely and, in the case of Para, that they did not occur. It might be mentioned in passing that such a system would, via ancestor rites, have ritualized publicly *all* of an individual's consanguineal ties over any period of several years and in so doing would have served to stress maximally the social opportunities or

options available to the individual through kinsmen (in a way that a more restrictive descent system probably would not).

16. See Price, *Maroon Societies; idem, The Guiana Maroons; idem, First-Time: The Historical Vision of an Afro-American People* (Baltimore and London: Johns Hopkins University Press, 1983).

17. The reasons why uterine rather than agnatic descent was chosen in this case requires a more complex explanation. It involved, we think, the great preponderance of men over women among the runaways, as well as the likely prevalence of the uterine principle in those African societies from which these people came. See Richard Price, *Alabi's World* (Baltimore and London: Johns Hopkins University Press, 1990).

18. Van Lier, *Frontier Society:* 159–60.

19. Wooding, *Winti:* 259–60; Van Lier, *Frontier Society:* 160.

20. Michael G. Smith, *Kinship and Community in Carriacou* (New Haven: Yale University Press, 1962).

21. *Ibid.,* 309–10.

22. Gabriel Debien, "La sucrerie Cottineau (1750–1777): Plantations et esclaves à Saint-Domingue." Université de Dakar, Publication de la Section d'Histoire no. 3, *Notes d'Histoire Coloniale* 66 (1962).

23. Fortes, "Introduction," in *The Developmental Cycle in Domestic Groups,* ed. Jack Goody (Cambridge: Cambridge University Press, 1958).

24. Matthew G. Lewis, *Journal of a West Indian Proprietor* (London: J. Murray, 1834): 258, cited in Patterson, *Sociology of Slavery:* 169–70.

25. Patterson *(ibid.,* 163) cites the evidence of one Henry Coor before a Select Committee on the Slave Trade (1790–1791): "It was not looked upon as anyways disadvantageous to an estate for the men to have a number of wives, from one, two, three or four, according as they had property to maintain them. What I mean by property is provisions on their little spots of ground . . ." Patterson quite reasonably points out that these relationships must have been reciprocal in some ways, else it would be difficult to explain why women were prepared to maintain them. The evidence is simply not complete enough for us to know whether polygynous unions were more common than monogamous unions; whether provision-grounds were distributed according to the nature of the union; whether domestic arrangements

were variable accordingly; and whether women held—as Patterson believes (*ibid.*, 169)—provision plots of their own.

26. Bryan Edwards, *The History, Civil and Commercial, of the British Colonies in the West Indies* (London, 1793), 2: 133.

27. Stewart, *A View:* 267; R. R. Madden, *A Twelvemonth's Residence in the West Indies* (London, 1835), 1: 136–37.

28. Long, *History of Jamaica* 2: 486–87; Mintz and Hall, *"Origins of the Jamaican system"*; Moreau de St. Méry, *Déscription . . . de la Partie Française,* 1: 433–36; Justin Girod de Chantrans, *Voyage d'un Suisse en différentes colonies* (Neuchatel, 1785): 131–32.

29. See, for instance, Long, *History of Jamaica* 2: 410–11; R. C. Dallas, *The History of the Maroons* (London, 1803), 1: cviii.

30. William Beckford, *A Descriptive Account of the Island of Jamaica* (London, 1790), 2: 151–87.

31. Patterson, *Sociology of Slavery:* 169.

32. *Ibid.*

33. William Davenport, "Introduction," *Social and Economic Studies* 10(4) (1961): 382.

34. Edith Clarke, "Land tenure and the family in four communities in Jamaica," *Social and Economic Studies* 1(4) (1953): 81–118; William Davenport, "The family system of Jamaica," *Social and Economic Studies* 10(4) (1961): 420–54.

35. Rémy Bastien, "Haitian rural family organization," *Social and Economic Studies* 10(4) (1961): 478–510.

36. Patterson, *Sociology of Slavery:* 167.

37. Herskovits, *Life in a Haitian Valley:* 260; Herskovits and Herskovits, *Trinidad Village:* 292. Edward Brathwaite, writing in a highly personal vein has noted:

I have seen girls in the markets of Port-au-Prince who are Yoruba or Dahomean market girls, except for the lack of tribal marks. The head-ties persist, some of the hairstyles persist, and the organization of markets—Kingston, Port-of-Spain, Castries, Port-au-Prince—are almost exact copies of markets in Lagos, Accra, Abomey, Ibadan. The specializations in these markets are similar and so is the segregation of the sexes. But one would need photographic and cinematic tape recordings to illustrate that the rhythms and sound-patterns of West Indian and West African markets are also similar. Both groups of markets are dominated by women who sit, squat, and socialize in similar ways, the head is used in the same way in both Africa and the Caribbean to carry baskets, trays and even small objects; gestures are similar; ways of attracting attention, arguing, bargaining, expressing pleasure, anger, flirtation, ridicule, are all similar. Even the colours of clothing and the choice of patterns and the way the dresses are worn—off the shoulder, rivered between the thighs when sitting—have clear resemblance on both sides of the Atlantic, though no comparative study of these and other essentials has yet been undertaken academically.

Edward Kamau Brathwaite, "Cultural diversity and integration in the Caribbean." Paper presented to the Schouler Lecture Symposium, The Johns Hopkins University, April 9–10, 1973 (n.d.): 38–39. We feel that these sensitive observations on market behavior, focused on what Brathwaite calls "the [trans-Atlantic] similarity of aesthetic taste and aesthetic response" (*ibid.*), are in much the same spirit as our earlier call for more careful ethnographic attention and historical analysis to be devoted to aesthetics and to other little-studied, somewhat abstract, but truly central aspects of cultural reality. Our own limited discussion of the role of female marketers here, however, is not intended to deal with the more subtle issues which Brathwaite's comments raise.

38. M. G. Smith, "African heritage": 42–43.

39. Sidney W. Mintz, "Les rôles économiques et la tradition culturelle," in *La femme de couleur en Amérique Latine*, ed. R. Bastide (Paris: Editions Anthropos, 1974): 115–48; *idem*, "Economic role and cultural tradition," in *The Black Woman Cross-Culturally*, ed. F. C. Steady (Boston: Schenkman, 1981): 513–34; *idem*, "Caribbean marketplaces and Caribbean history," *Radical History Review*, 27 (1982): 110–20. The Herskovitses themselves, writing of Trinidad (*Trinidad Village*: 292), noted that "Within the sphere of women's work, the phase most characteristically African is *not that women sell in the market, but that their earnings are their own*" (italics added).

40. The view of the nuclear family as an unsplittable economic atom (now more buffeted than ever before) is, then, itself an opinion, not gospel. Nevertheless, we believe that it has repeatedly accompanied "analyses" of the black family as a kind of intellectual ballast. Sidney W. Mintz, "Men, women, and trade," *Comparative Studies in Society and History* 13 (1971): 247–69.

7. CONCLUSION

1. C. Vann Woodward, "Clio with soul," *Journal of American History* 56 (1969): 17.

2. Herskovits, *Myth of the Negro Past:* 225.

BIBLIOGRAPHY

Abrahams, Roger D. "The shaping of folklore traditions in the British West Indies." *Journal of Inter-American Studies* 9 (1967): 456–80.

Alleyne, Mervyn C. "Acculturation and the cultural matrix of creolization." In Dell Hymes, ed., *Pidginization and Creolization of Languages*, 169–86. Cambridge: Cambridge University Press, 1971.

Alleyne, Mervyn C. *Roots of Jamaican Culture.* London: Pluto Press, 1988.

Armstrong, Robert P. *The Affecting Presence.* Urbana: University of Illinois Press, 1971.

Atwood, Thomas. *The History of the Island of Dominica.* London: J. Johnson, 1791.

Barbot, John. "A description of the coasts of North and South-Guinea." In Awnsham Churchill, ed., *A Collection of Voyages and Travels*, vol. 5. London, 1732.

Barnes, Sandra T., ed. *Africa's Ogun: Old World and New.* Bloomington: Indiana University Press, 1989.

Bascom, William R. "Two forms of Afro-Cuban divination." In Sol Tax, ed., *Acculturation in the Americas*, 169–79. Proceedings of the 29th International Congress of Americanists II. Chicago: University of Chicago Press, 1952.

Bastide, Roger. *Les religions africaines au Brésil.* Paris: Presses Universitaires de France, 1961.

Bastide, Roger. *Les Amériques noires*. Paris: Payot, 1967.

Bastide, Roger. *African Civilisations in the New World*. New York: Harper and Row, 1971.

Bastien, Rémy. "Haitian rural family organization." *Social and Economic Studies* 10 (1961): 478–510.

Beckford, William. *A Descriptive Account of the Island of Jamaica*. London: T. and J. Egerton, 1790.

Brathwaite, Edward Kamau. *The Development of Creole Society in Jamaica, 1770–1820*. Oxford: Clarendon Press, 1971.

Brathwaite, Edward Kamau. *Folk Culture of the Slaves in Jamaica*. London: New Beacon Books, 1981.

Brown, David H. *Garden in the Machine: Afro-Cuban Sacred Art and Performance in Urban New Jersey and New York*. Ph.D. dissertation, Yale University, 1989.

Bryce-Laporte, Roy S. "The slave plantation: background to present conditions of urban blacks." In P. Orleans and W. R. Ellis, eds., *Race, Change and Urban Society*, 265–66. Urban Affairs Annual Reviews 5. Beverly Hills: Sage, 1971.

Bryce-Laporte, Roy S. "Slaves as inmates, slaves as men: a sociological discussion of Elkins' thesis." In A. Lane, ed., *The Debate on Slavery*, 269–92. Urbana: University of Illinois Press, 1971.

Carr, Andrew. "A Rada community in Trinidad." *Caribbean Quarterly* 3 (n.d. [1953]): 35–54.

Clarke, Edith. "Land tenure and the family in four communities in Jamaica." *Social and Economic Studies* 1 (1953): 81–118.

Crowley, Daniel J. Review of S. Price and R. Price, *Afro-American Arts of the Suriname Rain Forest*, in *African Arts* 16 (1981): 27, 80–81.

Curtin, Philip. *The Atlantic Slave Trade: A Census*. Madison: University of Wisconsin Press, 1969.

Dalby, David. "The African element in American English." In T. Kochman, ed., *Rappin' and Stylin' Out: Communication in Urban Black America*, 170–86. Urbana: University of Illinois Press, 1972.

Dallas, R. C. *The History of the Maroons*. London: A. Strahan, 1803.

Dark, Philip J. C. *Bush Negro Art: An African Art in the Americas*. London: Tiranti, 1954.

Davenport, William. "The family system of Jamaica." *Social and Economic Studies* 10 (1961): 420–54.

Davenport, William. "Introduction." *Social and Economic Studies* 10 (1961): 378–85.

Debien, Gabriel. "Les engagés pour les Antilles (1634–1715)." *Revue d'Histoire des Colonies* 38 (1951).

Debien, Gabriel. "Les origines des esclaves des Antilles." *Bulletin de l'Institut Français d'Afrique Noire* 23, sér. B, nos. 3–4 (1961): 363–87.

Debien, Gabriel. "La sucrerie Cottineau (1750–1777): Plantations et esclaves à Saint-Domingue." Université de Dakar, Publication de la Section d'Histoire no. 3. *Notes d'Histoire Coloniale* 66 (1962).

Debien, Gabriel. "Les origines des esclaves des Antilles." *Bulletin de l'Institut Français d'Afrique Noire*, 27, sér. B. nos. 3–4 (1965): 755–99.

Debien, Gabriel. "Les origines des esclaves aux Antilles." *Bulletin de l'Institut Français d'Afrique Noire* 29, sér. B, nos. 3–4 (1967): 536–58.

DeCamp, David. "Introduction: The study of pidgin and creole languages." In Dell Hymes, ed., *Pidginization and Creolization of Languages*, 13–39. Cambridge: Cambridge University Press, 1971.

Delafosse, M., and Gabriel Debien. "Les origines des esclaves aux Antilles." *Bulletin de l'Institut Français d'Afrique Noire* 27, sér. B, nos. 1–2 (1965): 319–69.

Descourtilz, Michel. *Flore pittoresque et médicale des Antilles*. Paris: Rousselon, 1833.

Dillard, J. L. *Black Names*. The Hague: Mouton, 1976.

Edwards, Bryan. *The History, Civil and Commercial, of the British Colonies in the West Indies*. London: John Stockdale, 1793.

Elkins, Stanley. *Slavery: A Problem in American Institutional and Intellectual Life*. Chicago: University of Chicago Press, 1959.

Ellison, Ralph. *Shadow and Act*. New York: New American Library, 1966.

Fortes, Meyer. "Introduction." In Jack Goody, ed., *The Developmental Cycle in Domestic Groups*, 1–14. Cambridge Papers in Social Anthropology no. 1. Cambridge: Cambridge University Press, 1958.

Foster, George. "Peasant society and the image of limited good." *American Anthropologist* 67 (1965): 293–315.

Fouchard, Jean. *Les marrons de la liberté*. Paris: Editions de l'Ecole, 1972.

Frazier, E. Franklin *The Negro Family in the United States*. Chicago: University of Chicago Press, 1939.

Frazier, E. Franklin "The Negro in Bahia, Brazil: a problem in method." *American Sociological Review* 7 (1942): 465–78.

Gates, Henry Louis, Jr., *The Signifying Monkey: A Theory of Afro-American Literary Criticism*. New York: Oxford University Press, 1988.

Girod, François. *De la société créole (Saint-Domingue au 18ᵉ siècle)*. Paris: Hachette, 1972.

Girod de Chantrans, Justin. *Voyage d'un Suisse en différentes colonies*. Neuchatel: Impr. de la Société Typographique, 1785.

Goodenough, Ward H. *Description and Comparison in Cultural Anthropology*. Chicago: Aldine, 1970.

Greenfield, Sidney. "Socio-economic factors and family form." *Social and Economic Studies* 10 (1961): 72–85.

Hall, Douglas. "Slaves and slavery in the British West Indies." *Social and Economic Studies* 11 (1962): 305–318.

Hall, Gwendolyn M. *Social Control in Slave Plantation Societies*. Baltimore: Johns Hopkins University Press, 1971.

Handler, Jerome S. "The Amerindian slave population of Barbados in the seventeenth and early eighteenth centuries." *Caribbean Studies* 8 (1969): 38–64.

Handler, Jerome S., and Charlotte J. Frisbie. "Aspects of slave life in Barbados: music and its cultural context." *Caribbean Studies* 11 (1972): 5–40.

Harlow, V. T. *A History of Barbados, 1625–1685*. Oxford: Oxford University Press, 1926.

Herskovits, Melville J. "A preliminary consideration of the culture areas of Africa." *American Anthropologist* 26 (1924): 50–63.

Herskovits, Melville J. *Life in a Haitian Valley*. New York: Knopf, 1937.

Herskovits, Melville J. *Acculturation: The Study of Culture Contact*. New York: J. J. Augustin, 1938.

Herskovits, Melville J. "The Negro in Bahia, Brazil: a problem in method." *American Sociological Review* 8 (1943): 394–402.

Herskovits, Melville J. "Problem, method and theory in Afroamerican studies." *Afroamérica* 1 (1945): 5–24.

Herskovits, Melville J. *Man and His Works*. New York: Knopf, 1948.

Herskovits, Melville J. "Introduction." In Sol Tax, ed., *Acculturation in the Americas*, 48–63. Proceedings of the 29th International Congress of Americanists II. Chicago: University of Chicago Press, 1952.

Herskovits, Melville J. "Some psychological implications of Afroamerican studies." In Sol Tax, ed., *Acculturation in the Americas*, 152–60. Proceedings of the 29th International Congress of Americanists II. Chicago: University of Chicago Press, 1952.

Herskovits, Melville J. *The New World Negro*, ed. Frances S. Herskovits (Bloomington: Indiana University Press, 1966).

Herskovits, Melville J. "Some economic aspects of the Afrobahian Candomblé." In Frances S. Herskovits, ed., *The New World Negro*, 248–66. Bloomington: Indiana University Press, 1966.

Herskovits, Melville J. *The Myth of the Negro Past*. 1941; Boston: Beacon Press, 1990.

Herskovits, Melville J., and Frances S. Herskovits. *Suriname Folk-lore*. Columbia University Contributions to Anthropology, 27. New York: Columbia University Press, 1936.

Herskovits, Melville J., and Frances S. Herskovits. *Trinidad Village*. New York: Knopf, 1947.

Hoetink, Harry. *The Two Variants in Caribbean Race Relations*. London: Oxford University Press, 1967.

Holloway, Joseph E. "The origins of African-American culture." In Joseph E. Holloway, ed., *Africanisms in American Culture*, ix-xxi. Bloomington: Indiana University Press, 1990.

Houdaille, J. "Les origines des esclaves des Antilles." *Bulletin de l'Institut Français d'Afrique Noire* 25, sér. B, nos. 3–4 (1964): 601–675.

Houdaille, J., R. Massio, and G. Debien. "Les origines des esclaves des Antilles." *Bulletin de l'Institut Français d'Afrique Noire* 25, sér. B, nos. 3–4 (1963): 215–65.

Hurault, Jean. *Africains de Guyane: La vie matérielle et l'art des noirs réfugiés de Guyane*. The Hague: Mouton, 1970.

Hurbon, Laënnec. *Dieu dans le vaudou haïtien*. Paris: Payot, 1972.

Hymes, Dell. *Foundations in Sociolinguistics: An Ethnographic Approach*. Philadelphia: University of Pennsylvania Press, 1974.

Jackson, Walter. "Melville Herskovits and the Search for Afro-American

Culture." In George W. Stocking, Jr., ed., *Malinowski, Rivers, Benedict and Others: Essays on Culture and Personality*, 95–126. Madison: University of Wisconsin Press, 1986.

Jayawardena, Chandra. "Family organization in plantations in British Guiana." *International Journal of Comparative Sociology* 3 (1962): 63–64.

Joyner, Charles. "Creolization." In Charles Reagan Wilson and William Ferris, eds., *Encyclopedia of Southern Culture*, 147–49. Chapel Hill: University of North Carolina Press, 1989.

Joyner, Charles. "Speaking Southern," *New York Review of Books* (February 15, 1989): 52–53.

Kelly, J. *Voyage to Jamaica and Narrative of 17 years Residence in that Island*. Belfast: J. Wilson, 1838.

Kroeber, Alfred L. *Cultural and Natural Areas of Native North America*. University of California Publications in American Archeology and Ethnology, 38. Berkeley: University of California Press, 1939.

Labov, William. *Sociolinguistic Patterns*. Philadelphia: University of Pennsylvania Press, 1972.

Lane, Ann, ed. *The Debate on Slavery: Stanley Elkins and His Critics*. Urbana: University of Illinois Press, 1971.

Laurence, K. O. *Immigration into the West Indies in the 19th Century*. London: Caribbean Universities Press, 1971.

Leslie, Charles. *A New History of Jamaica*. London: J. Hodges, 1740.

Levine, Lawrence W. *Black Culture and Black Consciousness: Afro-American Folk Thought from Slavery to Freedom*. New York: Oxford University Press, 1977.

Lewis, Matthew G. *Journal of a West Indian Proprietor, Kept During a Residence in Jamaica*. London: J. Murray, 1834.

Lindblom, Gerhard. *Afrikanische Relikte und Indianische Entlehnungen in der Kultur der Busch-Neger Surinams*. Göteborg: Elanders Boktryckeri Aktiebolag, 1924.

Lloyd, P. C. *Africa in Social Change*. Baltimore: Penguin, 1972.

Lomax, Alan. "The homogeneity of African-Afro-American musical style." In N. Whitten and J. Szwed, eds., *Afro-American Anthropology*, 181–201. New York: Free Press, 1970.

Long, Edward. *The History of Jamaica*. London: T. Lowndes, 1774.

Madden, R. R. *A Twelvemonth's Residence in the West Indies*. London: James Cochrane, 1835.

Mannix, Daniel P., and Malcolm Cowley. *Black Cargoes: A History of the Atlantic Slave Trade*. New York: Viking, 1965.

Merriam, Alan P. "African music." In William R. Bascom and Melville J. Herskovits, eds., *Continuity and Change in African Cultures*, 49–86. Chicago: University of Chicago Press, 1959.

Miller, Joseph C. *Slavery: A Worldwide Bibliography, 1900–1982*. White Plains, NY: Kraus International, 1985.

Mintz, Sidney W. "The Jamaican internal marketing pattern." *Social and Economic Studies* 4 (1955): 95–103.

Mintz, Sidney W. "Cañamelar: the subculture of a rural sugar plantation proletariat." In J.H. Steward, *et al.*, eds., *The People of Puerto Rico*, 314–417. Urbana: University of Illinois Press, 1956.

Mintz, Sidney W. Review of S. Elkins, *Slavery*, in *American Anthropologist* 63 (1961): 579–87.

Mintz, Sidney W. "Currency problems in eighteenth-century Jamaica and Gresham's Law." In R. Manners, ed., *Patterns and Processes in Culture*, 248–65. Chicago: Aldine, 1964.

Mintz, Sidney W. "Slavery and the slaves." *Caribbean Studies* 8 (1969): 65–70.

Mintz, Sidney W. "Creating culture in the Americas." *Columbia University Forum* 13 (1970): 4–11.

Mintz, Sidney W. "Foreword." In N. Whitten and J. Szwed, eds. *Afro-American Anthropology: Contemporary Perspectives*. New York: Free Press, 1970.

Mintz, Sidney W. "Groups, group boundaries, and the perception of race." *Comparative Studies in Society and History* 13 (1971): 437–43.

Mintz, Sidney W. "Men, women, and trade." *Comparative Studies in Society and History* 13 (1971): 247–69.

Mintz, Sidney W. "The socio-historical background of pidginization and creolization." In Dell Hymes, ed., *Pidginization and Creolization of Languages*, 153–68. Cambridge: Cambridge University Press, 1971.

Mintz, Sidney W. "Toward an Afro-American history." *Cahiers d'Histoire Mondiale* 13 (1971): 317–32.

Mintz, Sidney W. "Les rôles économiques et la tradition culturelle." In R. Bastide, ed., *La Femme de couleur en Amérique Latine*, 115–48. Paris: Editions Anthropos, 1974.

Mintz, Sidney W. "Economic role and cultural tradition." In F. C. Steady, ed., *The Black Woman Cross- Culturally*, 513–34. Boston: Schenkman, 1981.

Mintz, Sidney W. "Caribbean marketplaces and Caribbean history." *Radical History Review* 27 (1982): 110–20.

Mintz, Sidney W. *Caribbean Transformations*. 1974; 2nd ed., New York: Columbia University Press, 1989.

Mintz, Sidney W., and Douglas Hall. "The origins of the Jamaican internal marketing system." In Sidney W. Mintz, ed., *Papers in Caribbean Anthropology*. New Haven: Yale University Publications in Anthropology 57, 1960.

Montero de Bascom, Berta. "Influencias africanas en la cultura cubana." *Ciencias Sociales* 5 (1954): 98-102.

Moreau de Saint- Méry, M. L. E. *Déscription...de la Partie Française de l'Isle Saint-Domingue*. 1797; Paris: Larose, 1958.

Newton, A. P. *The European Nations in the West Indies, 1493–1688*. London: A. & C. Black, 1933.

Nketia, J. H. "African music." In E.P. Skinner, ed., *Peoples and Cultures of Africa* 580–99. Garden City: Natural History Press, 1973.

Nugent, Lady Maria. *Lady Nugent's Journal*, ed. Frank Cundall. 1839; London: Institute of Jamaica, 1939.

Otterbein, Keith F. "Caribbean family organization: a comparative analysis." *American Anthropologist* 67 (1965): 66–79.

Patterson, Orlando. *The Sociology of Slavery*. London: MacGibbon and Kee, 1967.

Patterson, Orlando. "Slavery and slave revolts: A socio-historical analysis of the First Maroon War, Jamaica 1655–1740." *Social and Economic Studies* 19 (1970): 289–325.

Patterson, Orlando. *Die the Long Day*. New York: John Morrow, 1972.

Phillippo, James M. *Jamaica: Its Past and Present State*. London: John Snow, 1843.

Pollak-Eltz, Angelina. *Afro-Amerikaanse godsdiensten en culten*. Roermond: J. J. Romen en Zonen, 1970.

Price, Richard. "Saramaka emigration and marriage: a case study of social change." *Southwestern Journal of Anthropology* 26 (1970): 157–89.

Price, Richard. "Saramaka woodcarving: the development of an Afro-american art." *Man* 5 (1970): 363–78.

Price, Richard. "Studies of Caribbean family organization; problems and prospects." *Dédalo* 14 (1971): 23–59.

Price, Richard. "The Guiana maroons: changing perspectives in 'Bush Negro' studies." *Caribbean Studies* 11 (1972): 82–105.

Price, Richard, ed. *Maroon Societies: Rebel Slave Communities in the Americas*. 1973; 2nd ed., Baltimore: Johns Hopkins University Press, 1979.

Price, Richard. "KiKoongo and Saramaccan: A Reappraisal." *Bijdragen tot de Taal-, Land- en Volkenkunde* 131 (1975): 461–78.

Price, Richard. *Saramaka Social Structure: Analysis of a Maroon Society in Surinam*. Caribbean Monograph Series no. 12. Río Piedras: Institute of Caribbean Studies, 1975.

Price, Richard. *The Guiana Maroons: A Historical and Bibliographical Introduction*. Baltimore and London: Johns Hopkins University Press, 1976.

Price, Richard. *First-Time: The Historical Vision of an Afro-American People*. Baltimore and London: Johns Hopkins University Press, 1983.

Price, Richard. *Alabi's World*. Baltimore and London: Johns Hopkins University Press, 1990.

Price, Richard, and Sally Price. "*Kammbá*: the ethnohistory of an Afro-American art." *Antropologica* 32 (1972): 3–27.

Price, Richard, and Sally Price. "Saramaka onomastics: an Afro-American naming system." *Ethnology* 11 (1972): 341–67.

Price, Sally. *Co-Wives and Calabashes*. Ann Arbor: University of Michigan Press, 1984.

Price, Sally, and Richard Price. *Afro-American Arts of the Suriname Rain Forest*. Berkeley and Los Angeles: University of California Press, 1980.

Ramos, Arthur. *Las Culturas Negras en el Nuevo Mundo*. Mexico: Fondo de Cultura Económica, 1943.

Ranger, T. O. "Recent developments in the study of African religious and cultural history and their relevance for the historiography of the Diaspora." *Ufahamu* 4 (1973): 17–34.

Redfield, Robert, Ralph Linton, and Melville J. Herskovits. "Memorandum for the study of acculturation." *American Anthropologist* 38 (1936): 149–52.

Rinchon, Dieudonné. *Le trafic négrier*. Brussels: Atlas, 1938.

Rubin, V., ed. *Caribbean Studies: A Symposium*. Seattle: University of Washington Press, 1957.

Schumann, C. L. "Saramaccanisch Deutsches Wörter-Buch." In Hugo Schuchardt, ed., *Die Sprache der Saramakkaneger in Surinam*, 46–116. Verhandelingen der Koninklijke Akademie van Wetenschappen te Amsterdam 14 (1914).

Simey, T. S. *Welfare and Planning in the West Indies*. Oxford: Clarendon Press, 1946.

Simpson, George E. "Afro-American religions and religious behavior." *Caribbean Studies* 12 (1972): 5–30.

Simpson, George E., and P. B. Hammond. "Discussion." In V. Rubin, ed., *Caribbean Studies: A Symposium*, 46–53. Seattle: University of Washington Press, 1957.

Smith, Michael G. "The African heritage in the Caribbean." In V. Rubin, ed., *Caribbean Studies: A Symposium*, 34–46. Seattle: University of Washington Press, 1957.

Smith, Michael G. *Kinship and Community in Carriacou*. New Haven: Yale University Press, 1962.

Smith, Michael G. *West Indian Family Structure*. Seattle: University of Washington Press, 1962.

Smith, Raymond T. "The nuclear family in Afro-American kinship." *Journal of Comparative Family Studies* 1 (1970): 55–70.

Solien, Nancie L. "Household and family in the Caribbean." *Social and Economic Studies* 9 (1960): 101–106.

Staehelin, F. *Die Mission der Brüdergemeine in Suriname und Berbice im achtzehnten Jahrhundert*. Herrnhut: Vereins für Brüdergeschichte in Kommission der Unitätsbuchhandlung in Gnadau, 1913–1919.

Stedman, John Gabriel. *Narrative of a Five Years Expedition against the Revolted Negroes of Surinam*, ed. Richard Price and Sally Price. 1790; Baltimore and London: Johns Hopkins University Press, 1988.

Stewart, J. *A View of the Past and Present State of the Island of Jamaica*. Edinburgh: Oliver and Boyd, 1823.

Szwed, John F. "Afro-American musical adaptations." In N. Whitten and J. Szwed, eds. *Afro-American Anthropology*, 219–28. New York: Free Press, 1970.

Tannenbaum, Frank. *Slave and Citizen*. New York: Knopf, 1947.

Thompson, Robert F. "An aesthetic of the cool: West African dance." *African Forum* 2 (1966): 85–102.

Thompson, Robert F. "From Africa." *Yale Alumni Magazine* 34 (1970): 16–21.

Thompson, Robert F. *Black Gods and Kings*. Occasional Papers of the Museum and Laboratories of Ethnic Arts and Technology. Los Angeles: University of California, 1971.

Thompson, Robert F. "Recapturing heaven's glamour: Afro-Caribbean festivalizing arts." In John W. Nunley and Judith Bettelheim, eds., *Caribbean Festival Arts*, 17–29. Seattle: University of Washington Press, 1988.

Trouillot, Henock. "La condition des travailleurs à Saint-Domingue." *Revue de la Société Haïtienne d'Histoire, de Géographie et de Géologie* 34 (1969): 3–144.

Turner, Victor W. "Symbols in African Ritual." *Science* 179 (1973): 1100–1105.

Uchendu, Victor C. *The Igbo of Southeast Nigeria*. New York: Holt, Rinehart and Winston, 1965.

Van Lier, R. A. J. *Frontier Society: A Social Analysis of the History of Surinam*. Koninklijk Instituut voor Taal, Land en Volkenkunde, trans. ser. 14. The Hague: Martinus Nijhoff, 1971.

Volders, J. L. *Bouwkunst in Suriname: Driehonderd jaren nationale architectuur*. Hilversum: G. van Saane, 1966.

Voorhoeve, Jan. "Church creole and pagan cult languages." In D. Hymes, ed., *Pidginization and Creolization of Languages*. Cambridge: Cambridge University Press, 1971.

Voorhoeve, Jan, and Ursy M. Lichtveld. *Creole Drum: An Anthology of Creole Literature from Surinam*. New Haven: Yale University Press, 1975.

Waller, J. A. *A Voyage to the West Indies*. London: Sir Richard Phillips and Company, 1820.

Wood, Donald. *Trinidad in Transition*. London: Oxford University Press, 1968.

Wood, Peter H. " 'I did the best I could for my day': The study of early Black history during the Second Reconstruction, 1960 to 1976." *William & Mary Quarterly* 35 (1978): 185–225.

Wooding, Charles. *Winti: een Afroamerikaanse godsdienst in Suriname.* Meppel: Krips Repro., 1972.

Woodward, C. Vann. "Clio with soul." *Journal of American History* 61 (1969): 5–20.

Woodward, C. Vann. "The narcissistic South." *New York Review of Books* (October 26, 1989): 13–14, 16–17.

Woodward, C. Vann. "Rejoinder." *New York Review of Books* (February 15, 1990): 53.

INDEX

〰〰〰